# At the Beginning

Mary Matthews

First published in 2017 by
New Life Publishing,
Bedfordshire LU4 9HG

© Mary Matthews

British Library Cataloguing in Publication Data
A catalogue record for this book is available
from the British Library

ISBN   978 1 912237 03 6

All rights reserved.  No part of this book
may be reproduced, stored in a retrieval system,
or transmitted by any means – electronic, mechanical,
photocopying, recording or otherwise without the
prior written permission of the publishers.

Unless otherwise stated, Bible references are
from the New International Version © 1973,
The International Bible Society,
and are used with permission.

Typesetting by New Life Publishing,
Luton, UK   www.goodnewsbooks.co.uk
Printed and bound in Great Britain

# At the Beginning

## Mary Matthews

## Dedication

I want to dedicate this book to our dear friend Christine Noble, without whose pioneering work in making a way for women I, and many others, would not be doing the things we are doing today.

From the beginning of the Charismatic Movement, Christine pioneered prophetic dance and, even more importantly, women being released into ministry and leadership in the churches.

She was the first woman to speak from the platform at Spring Harvest.

She has taught and mentored women for many years; women who are now leading churches and filling other key roles in the Body of Christ.

This book would be incomplete without her.

### To protect my life I also have to mention my grandchildren

Gorgeous George
Delicious Dorothy
Delightful Demi
Beautiful Belle
and last but not least...
Buddy Blue Eyes.

I love you all very much!

# CONTENTS

Prologue ................................................................. 1
1. Climbing with my Boots on ................................. 5
2. Bible College and Park Avenue ......................... 13
3. Holywood and Carrickfurgus ............................ 21
4. Belfast Christian Family ..................................... 33
5. Des Dick's Story .................................................. 43
6. David Preston's Testimony ................................ 49
7. Janet Preston - Worship in Dance .................... 55
8. Pat Collins CM - That They May All ................ 59
9. John Noble - A God of Surprises ...................... 67
10. Charles Whitehead - The Surprises of the Spirit ....... 77
11. David's Story continued - Dallas, El Paso & Juarez ............ 85
12. Andy Au's Testimony ........................................ 93
13. Fr Peter Hocken - A Very English Way Into the
    Renewal of the Holy Spirit ................ 105
14. Myles Dempsey The Beginning of a New Dawn ......... 113
15. Sue Whitehead - Celebrate Legacy ............................ 129
16. Mary Matthews - Spring of Joy ................................. 135
Fr Peter Hocken, Memorial ............................................. 143

# PROLOGUE

2017 is perceived to be the fiftieth anniversary of Charismatic Renewal. At the end of the nineteenth century Pope Leo XIII was urged by a nun, Sr. Elena, to renew preaching and dedication to the Holy Spirit in the life of the church. She again urged the Pope in 1900 to begin the first year of the new century by praying 'Come Holy Spirit'. He wrote to the bishops twice to urge them to dedicate the twentieth century to the Holy Spirit and he spent the night of December 31st 1899 alone in the Vatican praying for this intention.

We now know that within a few hours God's first response fell on a group of Methodists in Topeka, Kansas. They too were praying that night to understand the events described in the Acts of the Apostles and the Holy Spirit touched the whole group – with a new fire and an anointing to pray in tongues. This is generally seen as the beginning of the Pentecostal Church. In 1904/1905 the Welsh Revival broke out and in 1906 the Holy Spirit fell in Asuza Street, in Los Angeles, and it was the beginning of the Pentecostal Movement.

In January of 1936, David Du Plessis, a Pentecostal Pastor in South Africa was visited unexpectedly by Smith Wigglesworth a Pentecostal evangelist known as the 'apostle of faith' who moved in signs and wonders and even raised people from the dead. Wigglesworth pushed him against a wall and said the following:

> 'There is a revival coming that at present the world knows nothing about. It will come through the churches. It will come in a fresh way. When you see what God does in this revival you will then have to admit that what you have seen previously is a mere nothing in comparison with what is to come. It will eclipse anything that has been known in history. Empty churches, empty cathedrals will be packed again with worshippers. Buildings will not be able to accommodate the multitudes. Then you will see fields of people worshipping and praising together.

In 1959, Pope John XXIII called the Second Vatican Council, and dedicated it to the Holy Spirit. His opening prayer at the Council was 'Renew Thy Wonders in this our day as by a new Pentecost.' What has followed in the last fifty plus years is the greatest renewal of the whole church and greater unity among Christians since the early church in the book of Acts.

I have not set out to write this book as a precise historical record of what took place in Northern Ireland and the rest of the British Isles at the beginning of what has become known on the Catholic side as Charismatic Renewal and on the Protestant side as the Charismatic Movement. I have rather wanted to bring together the memories of some of the people who were there 'At the

Beginning' (Acts 11:15-17) and who experienced the amazing move of God's Spirit across these islands. People like Charles Whitehead, John Noble, Fr. Pat Collins and particularly my husband, David Matthews. I shared something of my own experiences in the book 'In the Valley', which was more of my personal story and told something of the 'cost' people paid to follow God in this movement.

This time I want to share much more of the 'Glory and the Joy' of what happened to us especially from the perspective of my husband David who was involved personally with both sides, with the Protestant Charismatic Movement and the Roman Catholic Charismatic Renewal.

We have many friends who were with us in those experiences 'At the beginning' who have also shared something of their own remembrances of those days. Most of these events took place in the nineteen sixties, seventies, and eighties. I have been blessed and excited as I have written this book remembering the wonderful things that happened. The fulfilment of Wigglesworth's prophetic word can be seen across these islands; for example in Westminster Central Hall an ancient church filled with worshipping people who came together from Roman Catholic and Protestant backgrounds in the nineteen eighties.

Even on the South Coast of England where we now live we see 'thousands of people worshipping together in fields', in events such as Church Big Day Out and David's Tent, to name but a few near us. People meet in the Celebrate and New Dawn Conferences plus others in Birmingham, Liverpool and many other places. Churches that have lain empty are being filled with worshipping Spirit filled Christians in many centres across the country as in St. Peters in Brighton a church plant from Holy Trinity Brompton, an Anglican church in London and the home of the Alpha Course, all as a result of the Charismatic Movement.

My prayer for this book is that we will be led together once more to pray Pope John XX111's prayer for our day and time, 'Renew Thy Wonders in this our day as by a new Pentecost.'

**Lord Let Your Glory Fall!**

*Mary Matthews, 2017*

# ONE

## CLIMBING WITH MY BOOTS ON

## DAVID'S STORY

Mary and I were both born in Belfast Northern Ireland in the late nineteen forties. Some of my very earliest memories are of my granny taking me to church. My parents were healthy pagans, but they believed that their boys should go to church and Sunday School and my granny, a very godly woman, took us there. Even at that early age I had a real hunger for God and was aware of His Presence.

I can remember sitting on those wooden chairs before service started everyone bowing their heads. When I was about six or seven years old I bowed my head with the others. My twin brother Roddy dug me in the ribs and said, 'Davesy Boy what are you doing?' I replied, 'I don't know but everybody else is doing it.'

That was my introduction to prayer and later I became very fond of the prayer meetings in church and especially the half-nights of prayer, which were on Friday night going on to the early hours Saturday morning.

My Pastor, Mr Anderson, one night said something to me

that I didn't understand at the time. 'David when you pray something happens, a Presence comes, please keep praying', but I had no idea what that meant.

The church we went to was on the Crumlin Road in Belfast. It was part of the Free Methodist Church of North America, an evangelical denomination in the Methodist tradition. They taught Methodist doctrines and we sang a lot of Charles Wesley's hymns, which I loved. They were so full of spiritual truths. If we felt excited by the words we were singing we took out our hankies and waved them in the air. That was as demonstrative as it got.

The gifts of the Spirit were never mentioned in my church. No one ever taught that there even *were* gifts of the Spirit and they were available for today. The emphasis was on preaching and teaching and a fundamental belief in The Bible as the Word of God, which I have been grateful for ever since.

I preached my first sermon there at the age of twelve at the funeral of my Sunday School teacher. He was a godly man who had worked in Harland and Wolfe Shipyard all his life. The thing I remember him for most was that he would always say, 'David, I want to die with my boots on'.

I also greatly admired my Pastor, Carl Anderson, a Godly man who often said to me, 'David, when I die, I want to die climbing'. Those words put something into me as a boy. I used to think, 'I want to be like these men. I don't ever want to give up or walk away from God or sit on my hands and say, 'this is far enough, or this is good enough.' I want to die climbing with my boots on!'

These people planted in me the seeds that made me hungry for the Baptism in the Spirit and put into me the idea that I wanted everything that God could give me, and in that way I owe a deep debt of gratitude to them.

Then I met my wife, Mary, in the spring of 1965. I heard about a youth group called Christians in Action which was full of enthusiastic young people with a passion to share their Christian faith, the Good News of the Gospel'; so I went along. The inspirational scriptural motto of the group was Acts 1:8

> 'For ye shall receive power after the Holy Spirit has come upon you and you shall be witnesses unto Me in Jerusalem, Judea, Samaria and unto the uttermost parts of the earth.'

The unfortunate thing was that we had the 'witnesses' part right but not the power of the Holy Ghost part. We didn't have the power of the Spirit, 'dynamos', the dynamite power that Jesus promised us would impact the world and change people's lives. We had not 'clothed ourselves with power from on high.'

As a matter of fact the Baptism of the Holy Spirit was frowned upon in our group. One of the leaders clearly told us that we didn't need the Gift of Tongues because we didn't praise Jesus enough with the tongue we had.

So every night we went out into the city of Belfast holding open-air gospel services handing our leaflets to people and talking to them about the 'Good News.' The problem was that the good news we were sharing was not very good news for people. Jesus met people at the point of their need; we met everyone at the same point:

> 'You are all sinners and the wages of sin is death. Jesus died for you and if you repent He will forgive your sin and you won't have to go to hell when you die.'

Not such good news really when there was so much more. But it was all we knew at the time.

A Baptist chap called Ron Pinder began to come along to the group. He had just been baptised in the Holy Spirit and was absolutely passionate about the experience. He talked to me about it constantly and I thought he was crazy and showed no real interest. However the desire to follow God anywhere at any cost was still very strong in me.

I had got hold of a little book called 'The Cross and the Switchblade' by an American Pentecostal Minister called David Wilkerson. This book told the marvellous story of gangland drug addicts in New York being baptised in the Holy Spirit, and speaking in tongues. These troubled young people were then set free from drugs and became dynamic preachers and evangelists.

I thought, 'I want this!' It was a most marvellous move of God and in many ways helped pave the way for the much wider Charismatic Movement which came later, in the historic churches. So I read this book and thought, 'If I have this it will help me to preach and share the gospel.' So I talked to Ron.

Ron and I went to a private room in the house where the group met, to pray for Baptism in the Spirit. My idea was that I would get baptised in the Holy Spirit, speak in tongues once to confirm it and then get on with evangelism. Ron was very nervous because I had been so adamant about how wrong he was about this whole tongues thing. I am not sure if he even took me seriously, so he just talked and talked.

He must have talked at least thirty minutes; it felt like an hour, trying to explain to me about speaking in tongues. I switched off halfway through thinking, this is a waste of time. I was shouting inside; 'Ron I'm ready, just lay hands on me and let's get on with it.'

It seemed that one of the essential elements in receiving the Holy Spirit was that someone laid hands on you, because that's how they did it in the Bible. By the time Ron did that I was emotionally dry. I think for me that was a good thing because I am quite an emotional person. But at that time I was emotionally empty thinking, 'this is not going to work, it is pointless.'

And he prayed and nothing happened, and he kept praying and

while he was praying I felt God was speaking to me. It was rather strange He said, 'I want you to take off your coat.'

I'd been a suit and tie man all my life and I remember thinking, Lord I know there are only two of us but this is still a meeting; it would be a bit inappropriate to take off my jacket. But this thought persisted and rather reluctantly I took off my jacket folded it neatly and laid it across the bed.

Immediately I was baptised in the Holy Spirit. Tongues were flying out of my mouth. I forgot about the idea of doing it just once. I couldn't stop speaking in tongues, they just kept flowing and flowing. After a long time I had enough self-awareness to stagger onto my feet and put my jacket back on.

Then I did two things; I had promised the Lord that if He baptised me in the Holy Spirit I would stay up till two o clock to pray. Also by this time Mary and I were 'going steady', so the other thing was that I needed to go to see her because I knew if I just laid hands on her she would be baptised in the Spirit too, so I made my way up to Mary's house and told her what had happened. Maybe it was my wild eyes or something, but I was about to lay hands on her when she said: 'Whatever you've got, I don't want it, Leave me alone.'

And God told me to leave her alone. I came home to pray, with this eternity until two o clock in the morning stretching before me, then I thought I should read up on these tongues in the Bible to make sure they are in there and eventually found 1 Corinthians 12, 13, and 14.

Chapter 13 I was very familiar with, 12 a bit, but 14 was new ground for me and I started reading it and thought 'Well that's all right, tongues is in the Bible' and then I read on and it said, *'It's better to prophecy.'*

> 1 Corinthians 14:1-5
> *'Pursue love and desire spiritual gifts, but especially that you may prophecy, for he who speaks in a tongue edifies himself, but he who prophesies edifies the church.*
>
> *I wish you all spoke with tongues but even more that you prophesied for he who prophesises is greater than he who speaks in tongues unless indeed he interprets so that the church may be edified.'*

I am a Biblicist; I believe the truth of the Bible so if Paul says its better to prophecy than to speak in tongues I know that must be right. So I began to prophecy. Prophetic words just rolled out of me. Then I read

> *'I will sing with my understanding and I will sing with my spirit'*

And I said, 'I don't know what this is but it's in the Bible so I'll have this as well.'

I had an old Presbyterian hymn book belonging to Granny Matthews in the house, and I picked up my granny's hymnbook and sang a hymn - just a good Presbyterian hymn. I sang it in English. I didn't know that with tongues you had to make up your own tune as well so this time I used the same tune and instead of singing it in English, I sang in tongues.

I managed to pray in tongues, sing in tongues and read the scriptures till two in the morning and then I went to bed. I thought 'I've done what I said I would. And that's that.'

If I'd known then the enormity of what I'd done, I might have backed out, but I decided to carry on climbing with my boots on!

# TWO

# BIBLE COLLEGE AND PARK AVENUE

Because of his discernment of the anointing that came when I prayed, Pastor Anderson felt that I should become a Pastor in the Free Methodist Church. I had already helped pioneer a church plant with my Uncle Bill in East Belfast and was preaching regularly.

His advice threw me a bit because my mum always thought that my brothers and I should be schoolteachers because teachers always had secure employment in those days and my poor dad had been out of work a lot during our childhood. Mum's greatest ambition for her children was to give them an education so that we would have good jobs and not face periodic redundancy.

So I had teaching in my heart so that financially I would be secure and later on 'we' would be secure so when Pastor came up with this idea that I should be a Pastor I said to him, 'No I don't think that's right, I want to become a schoolteacher.' Well he said 'Lets wait and I'll pray about it'.

Over the next few years, his prayers seemed to be stronger than my desire to be a schoolteacher and I ended up pursuing the idea of doing a three year ministerial course at a Seminary or Bible College as we called them in those days - Emmanuel Bible

College in Birkenhead across the Mersey from Liverpool. Emmanuel was a very traditional Holiness Bible College established at the beginning of the century to train missionaries to work in Africa, India, and South America. I studied Greek, philosophy and theology but the regime was tough, involving hard physical work both in the gardens and on the building. They were training young people for a life in third world countries where they would have to provide basic infrastructures as well as preaching the gospel. One summer I even helped to put a new roof on the college.

I wasn't able to carry on enjoying baptism in the Spirit at that time or having fellowship with others of the same mind. To me Baptism in the Spirit was a very personal thing. It was my experience and I didn't feel the need to promote it. It was something that had happened to me. I was still speaking in tongues but it was private and devotional.

When I got to Bible College the atmosphere was heavy and legalistic and I lost the joy of Baptism in the Spirit. Eventually I lost the ability to speak in tongues; or seemingly lost it. I also was battling with depression. I kept asking God to baptise me in the Spirit again to lift me out of this darkness and the effect of my dour surroundings and poor food. I felt as I prayed and even fasted at times that God said to me', 'I will not do what I have already done'.

I shared a bedroom with three other men. The only way I could get privacy to pray was to put my head under the blankets.

One day I put my head under the blankets and said 'Lord I accept that I am baptised in the Spirit and I will speak in tongues.' So with no great emotion I did that.

And of course when I was baptised in the Spirit initially one of the things I read in Corinthians was that Paul said, He who speaks in tongues should pray that he will interpret. I had interpreted that night. Now in Bible College under the blankets I spoke in tongues and was given the interpretation of what I was saying. Words of courage, words of strength and encouragement, things that began to build me up in my faith and in the things of the Spirit.

While was in college I heard about the 'Full Gospel Businessmen's Fellowship International.' This was a fellowship of mainly American, Spirit-filled men who came to Britain to hold a Convention in November 1965. Many British leaders of the charismatic movement attended this conference and there was a lot of media interest in it.

And I had a question; and my question was this: could you receive all nine gifts of the Spirit? And these men looked like the people who could answer my question. So I wrote to Demos Shakarian who was the leader of the group, because I thought I might as well go to the top man, he should know. I had a lovely reply, which I kept for many years, from his secretary, a chap called Jewel Rose who didn't say, 'David don't be silly or David go for all nine.'

He said 'David, I am convinced that God will give you every gift of the Sprit that is necessary for you to fulfil the calling that God has put on your life.'

That was great wisdom. I was content with that. I think in my life since then I have seen every gift of the Spirit operate in me and through me, by the grace of God, some only rarely but others regularly. This made me open to the Holy Spirit and determined once again to at any cost, or all cost, to follow the Lord and the promptings of His Holy Spirit.

While I was at Bible College, unknown to me there was this world-wide move of the Holy Spirit beginning to take place and I remember at one prayer meeting one of the students had the audacity to pray in tongues. She was eventually expelled from the college. I was concerned and confused and thought. 'What do I do?'

I pointed out to my theology tutor that the Bible was clear, it said 'forbid not to speak in tongues.' He just ignored it and said, you leave that to us, but if you speak in tongues you'll be expelled. For whatever reason, good or bad, I didn't feel that I should challenge that and I should continue to keep tongues as a personal experience between me and God, get through Bible College and get into what I really wanted to do, which was to be a Pastor.

After college I came home to Belfast and took up my first pastorate in the little church plant that my uncle and I had founded together in East Belfast some years before. I was appointed as Pastor to the church and the Free Methodist Church ordained me and they liked their pastors to wear clerical collars and so I was duly fitted out. Six months later on January 18th 1969 Mary and I were married in her little Anglican church in the presence of our loving families and many friends. I was twenty two years old and Mary was twenty.

The church had bought a large house which was converted to accommodate what the Americans liked to call the sanctuary downstairs and a two bedroom flat for us to live in upstairs, so we lived above the job. There was plenty of room for growth as there were only about six people in the congregation in a room that held fifty. Before each service I went round the room praying over each seat asking God to fill it and bless the person who sat in it. I did that for the prayer meeting as well. I put fifteen chairs out initially praying that there would be fifteen people in the prayer meeting.

The Holy Spirit began to move. In the houses right around the church, people were converted and their lives changed. One night in the prayer meeting fourteen seats were filled and there was one empty one. To our amazement Harry from across the street, a man with many problems and many difficulties, walked in and filled the empty seat. Then he got converted, what a happy night. I remember once a visiting preacher encouraged us to sing loudly so that the people across the street would hear us and maybe come to church. What he didn't know was that most of the people from across the street were already in the church.

Then one night in our prayer meeting it all kicked off. I'd kept this baptism in the Spirit thing to myself, I spoke in tongues, I didn't expect anybody else to, or try to promote it in any way whatsoever. We had a practice in the prayer-meeting of going to one another and praying for requests, for jobs, for healing, or for anything else people needed.

On this particular night I felt I should go and pray with Ginny Marshall a lovely lady who lived in the Prefabs; 'temporary' homes for people who were homeless after the blitz twenty five years before. I went to her and began to pray for healing because I thought if God wants me to pray for her she must be sick. Then I felt the Lord say to me she isn't sick, pray for her deliverance. I didn't know what that meant but if God tells you to do something you do it.

I prayed that Ginny would be delivered and that God would bless her. The next thing I knew was that Ginny Marshall was speaking in tongues absolutely fluently. I thought, 'Now what do I do,' and I tried to move on. Then others began to be filled with the Spirit and some of them became 'drunk' in the Spirit.

I came out of that prayer meeting knowing two things: one, this was a move of the Spirit and I dare not resist it and two, this is going to cost me everything - and it did. We were thrown out of the church and with my job went our income and home.

When I say people were drunk in the Spirit I mean they were

acting like 'drunken' people just as believers were on the Day of Pentecost. There was one young man who lived just across the road and I had to help him down the drive and across the street and into his home because he couldn't stand up on his own. So Ginny was delivered and people were healed and I sat there in fear.

Ginny told me afterwards that for months every time she had tried to pray she felt as if she was choking, and when she tried to read the Bible she heard awful blasphemies in her mind, swear words that Ginny would never have used and again this choking sensation. In her words she said 'When we prayed in that prayer meeting the choking left me.' Then she was so free that the Holy Spirit began to flow through her and out of her.

We had some wonderful times in those prayer meetings. When I was first baptised in the Spirit the Lord told me not to go to any Pentecostal churches or read any Pentecostal books. The main reason I did that was that I didn't want anyone to say that I had received this experience from the Pentecostal meetings I knew I had received it from God and had it confirmed from the Bible. I wanted to be able to say, 'I searched the scriptures for myself and found these things to be true.'

We had prophetic words and visions and all kinds of things that for us became just part of praying for one another. God had taken over and the Holy Spirit was moving. Some students and other young people who had been part of Mary's youth group in her Anglican church had begun to join us and bring other friends along. Her younger brother, Jim, came along and was wonderfully baptised in the Holy Spirit. We had late nights of prayer at the weekend where some of these young men worshipped and prayed in the Spirit far into the night.

# THREE

# HOLYWOOD AND CARRICKFERGUS

## On the Sides of the North

Our little daughter Avril had been born in April and was diagnosed immediately after birth with something called congenital hip condition. It was diagnosed by our wonderful G.P. and she was fitted with a brace that held her thighs in a horizontal position.

'I am afraid Avril will have to wear this brace for at least a year' the consultant said 'and probably longer'.

There were a few visiting speakers coming to us from England and one of them had particular healing gifts so when Avril was two months old we held a healing service in church and after our baby was prayed for we both had a deep conviction from God and we knew that God had healed her. It wasn't that we tried to convince ourselves or 'name it and claim it!'

The Holy Spirit was moving in power and we just knew without a doubt that the Lord had healed Avril. We carried on using the brace however until our next visit to the consultant. At the next hospital appointment the doctors ordered further x-rays and scratched their heads.

'Well I don't know what has happened but her condition no longer shows on her x-rays. Come for one more visit and if things are the same we will discharge her.' We knew what had happened! Praise God!

The church had grown so much that The Free Methodists wanted to build a larger building and I was called to a meeting thinking they wanted to discuss it. But they wanted to talk about me and what was happening in the church. Somehow news had got back to them.

'This is not the 'image or ethos of our church' the Bishop said. We think you would be happier in a Pentecostal Church.' And the deal they put to me was this, I could stay on as Pastor as long as I never preached about the gifts of the Spirit and tongues, which I never had done.

At that time Avril was two months old so I came home to my wife, to my lovely Mary, and I said to her, 'here is the deal,' and I was willing to take to deal. It is a big responsibility to be married and to have a child.

'We can stay here as long as I put this whole thing in my back pocket and sit on it never speak or preach about the Baptism in the Spirit and stop these things from happening in the services.' I will never ever forget what she said to me and she has held true to this for all these years:

> 'If I ever hear you preach something you don't believe in, I will get up and leave'.

And so we were given the 'right boot of fellowship.' In those days being 'charismatic' was not the acceptable thing that it is today. We were really pioneering along with many others and through time this would open the way for people in the wider church to come into these experiences. However at this point it cost us everything.

With the job went our income and our home. The flat came with the pastorate and I was untrained for any other profession although I had worked in the Civil Service during my gap year. I now knew without a doubt that God had called me to be a pastor in His church.

And we were out, with a new baby, no home, no prospects and no money.

We had just met a Pentecostal pastor called Keith Gerner who was about to start a Bible College in Holywood, Co. Down. A number of students had already enrolled and I was invited to become a member of staff which provided us with a home and some work. I accepted the offer even though I knew that whatever I was, I was not a Pentecostal, as I could not adhere to Pentecostal doctrine and could not join the Pentecostal Church.

When I was baptised in the Spirit the Lord had told me not to read Pentecostal books but to study the Holy Spirit straight from the Bible and especially from the Book of Acts.

The Bible College was in a big old house in the Holywood hills, it was actually two large houses that had been knocked through into one. During that time I taught seminars in the day and travelled every night to little Pentecostal Fellowships around Northern Ireland to generate an income.

During that year there was a speaker called Hugh Thompson at the Christmas Conference. Hugh was a House Church Leader from Bristol. House church was new to me but many of them had sprung up across England with people in similar situations to our own who had been baptised in the Holy Spirit but were not Pentecostal. Some were Baptists others Brethren, Salvation Army, or Methodist. The Holy Spirit was moving in all denominations.

Hugh was from a Brethren background and had been baptised in the Holy Spirit in 1964. The general conviction of the House Church groups was that the restoration of the gifts of the Spirit was in order that the church would be reconstituted as a vibrant and effective fellowship of believers functioning as the Body of Christ as they did in the New Testament church. The emphasis was on Body Ministry and being in committed relationships with one another.

I got on well with Hugh and became very interested in what was happening in groups like his and others in England. We were struggling living in the Bible College with our young baby and I knew that God had more for us, so after a year I knew that He was moving us on once more and the next part of our story began.

We prayed and once again God miraculously provided for us. New housing estates were being built in towns outside Belfast to help ease the situation in the city. Many people were moving because of the Troubles which were rumbling on in Northern Ireland. My own parents moved to a safer area in a housing estate in Bangor and Mary's parents moved to Lisburn, County Antrim.

I had indicated to the housing authority that we would be without a home at the end of the school year and were allocated a brand new council house in Carrickfergus, a little town by the sea, north of Belfast.

I continued to study the Bible to find out more about the things of the Holy Spirit that we were experiencing. The Lord began to speak to me from the Book of Acts. I saw things like, how the early Christians lived in community, meeting in each others homes. I saw from Corinthians how each had their own individual gifting and part to play in serving the Family of God, exercising their gifts as they met together.

So I spent the next three years 'in the wilderness' being taught by the Holy Spirit about all of these things and metaphorically 'making tents' to earn a living, as the apostle Paul did.

I had to earn money to pay the rent and provide for my growing family; Mary was now expecting our second child. First of all I took a job cleaning cars in a local garage. As I had experience working in the Civil Service, I then got a job as a clerk in the office of Courtaulds factory nearby. Courtaulds produced synthetic fibres from chemicals which were then used to make all kinds of products.

There was a very large element of living by faith involved as well, as we trusted God for our needs. Often when the money for the rent was due on Monday morning, someone would put an envelope through our door on Sunday night with just the right amount of money to cover the payment.

We began to meet for worship with some friends and to have fellowship in our home and over a period of time others began to join us in our little group. And in this way our little 'house church' began. We found out more about the Christians in England who had been taught the same things as we were being taught by the Holy Spirit. Some had to leave their church denominations in the same way as we had. Many of them had been meeting in small groups in each other's homes.

One day I was praying and the Holy Spirit gave me a vision of a row of small back yards similar to the ones in the kind of houses my granny had lived in. These back yards had high brick walls separating them but no doors. And in each yard someone was shouting, 'We are all one in Christ, we are all one in Christ.' I thought, if we are all one in Christ why someone doesn't climb over the wall into the next yard. The Holy Spirit said to me 'Why don't you?'

A young Anglican priest and his family lived around the

corner from us. His name was Eric. I had met him somewhere in the town but had made no effort to get to know him. Now I had a strong urge to visit him.

I rang the doorbell and when he opened it he looked very tired and dishevelled. We talked for a while and he told me he had been praying for weeks that someone would come to help him. He was deeply depressed and felt that he had lost his faith.

We talked a bit more about the things of the Spirit and eventually he asked me to pray. I laid hands on him and he was wonderfully baptised in the Holy Spirit. Soon after his wife Sheila came home from work and also asked for prayer. She was beautifully baptised in the Holy Spirit as well.

The four of us became firm friends.

During our time in Holywood we had met a couple called Mike and Penny Stevens. Mike was a captain in the Parachute Regiment which was based near us at Holywood Barracks. They were part of a group of house churches lead by Bryn Jones in the North of England. They were looking for fellowship during their posting in Northern Ireland and they came to the meetings in the Bible College when they could. We also became friends and sometimes went for a meal in their army house at the barracks.

I was invited to attend a conference with Bryn Jones where I would meet some of these other 'house-church' leaders in England. There was only one problem: I didn't have the money to pay for the travel expenses, so we prayed about it!

Mike heard of my plans and obeyed the Lord's prompting to help us. He sent us a cheque for enough money to cover the family's expenses for the three weeks I would be away. It was dated for two days after the date I was to leave which left me with fifty pence for travel expenses.

I was launched into my greatest faith adventure to date. I set off for England with fifty pence in my pocket hitching a ride to the ferry port of Larne and once again I prayed.

The Lord led me to go to a particular lorry and ask the driver if he was going to England. The driver laughed and said 'England is a big place', but it turned out that this man was travelling to Birmingham, the city where I was to meet Bryn Jones.

'Have you got a ticket for the boat'? The man asked. I was a bit embarrassed, I had forgotten that I would need a passenger ticket in order to travel on the ferry. 'Oh that's all right,' the driver said. 'I have plenty of them, get in!'

The lorry was owned by a company called 'Duke's' based in Portadown. Since then many times when we have been in need of a sign of God's faithfulness and provision, we have seen a Dukes Transport lorry travelling on the roads of England. We also now have a miniature model of a 'Dukes lorry' in our sitting room and bought one for each of our children, to remind us of God's goodness, faithfulness and provision.

On arrival in Birmingham I spent my 50p on accommodation in a doss house and next day was met by Bryn Jones who picked me up in his car and took me to the conference where I met many of these house church leaders. There was great unity among them all at that time and I was greatly encouraged in the Spirit.

I met men like Graham Perrins from Cardiff, John Noble and Maurice Smith from Romford in Essex, Peter Parris from Bradford, Gerald Coates, Arthur Wallis and many others. After the conference I went on to visit a number of these house church groups and came home with a few pounds in my pocket, gifts for preaching.

Over the next few years I visited Hugh in Bristol and Peter Parris in Bradford, having exposure to these different groups and seeing what the Holy Spirit was doing. I visited John Noble and his group in Romford. At that time they had outgrown a house and were meeting in a pub called the Cauliflower. I was drawn to John as a mentor. He was very wise and full of integrity.

We then had a number of English house church leaders visit us in Carrickfergus. We were such a small insignificant group it was miraculous that they came. Among them were Wally North and Norman Meeten who lead groups in Liverpool and the North West. I had heard Wally North preach at a large house I used to visit in Bible College days in the Wirral and enjoyed his Holy Spirit Wesleyan style ethos.

We now planned a family trip to visit them in Liverpool. The marked feature of their groups was the worship. Almost exclusively they sang Wesleyan hymns. They used a hymn book called Hymns of Eternal Truth, the complete unedited hymns of Charles Wesley. These hymns are full of tremendous scriptural and spiritual truths, such as in the Christmas Hymn. The line that always sticks with me is the amazingly concise Incarnational Truth:

*'Our God contracted to a span, incomprehensibly made man'*

What amazing words and every hymn contains these amazing theological insights. In Liverpool they were sung at great length with great gusto!

We carried on down to Bristol to Hugh Thompson's group and spent some days with them, an entirely different kind of fellowship and worship but moving in the same gifts and power of the Holy Spirit. Later we also visited Peter Parris in Bradford, a group similar to Hugh's, they were both part of the Bryn Jones stream of churches.

I began to know in my spirit that this is where God was leading our little group, a house church not necessarily the same as any of the ones I had seen but similar and completely unique. Little did I know just how unique our group would be!

I then began to feel the leading of the Holy Spirit to move back into the city of Belfast and we moved from Carrickfergus into

Belfast in 1973 taking our little house church with us, the first one in Ireland! Once again God miraculously provided for us, giving us a large house in Ravenhill Park next door to the Ulster Rugby Grounds, at the ridiculously low rent of £10 per week. Our friend David Preston who had been meeting with us in Carrick moved in with us and became the first of many single people who lived in our extended family.

By faith God had given us a vision for the spiritual city within the city, He was calling us to help build His City and soon there were others being born into it as they experienced the move of Holy Spirit. (Psalm 48).

Soon after we moved we discovered that friends of ours from Mary's old church days were living just down the street. They were continuing to meet with others from the group who had been baptised in the Holy Spirit, even though we had been out of touch with them for a number of years. They had been living together in the west of the province and also had recently moved back to the city.

The Lord spoke to me and said that they were like sheep without a shepherd and I was like a shepherd without sheep. So with great joy we came together again! We began to meet in our new home and very soon even more people joined us; mostly young people who were being baptised in the Holy Spirit.

Another couple, Charlie and Marjorie Houston rented another large house across the street from us with their children and a number of single people. We became a community as others moved into the area. Our worship was led by a couple of guys on guitar and David on the bongo drums. One of our members, Ronnie Wilson, wrote many songs at that time and some of them were prophetic.

> *'I hear the sound of rustling in the leaves of the trees,*
> *The Spirit of the Lord has come down on the earth,*
> *The church that seemed in slumber has now risen from its knees*
> *And dry bones respond with the fruits of new birth.*
> *And this is not a phase which is passing*
> *It's the start of an age that is to come.'*
> *And where is the wise man and the scoffer*
> *Before the face of Jesus they are dumb.*
> *My tongue is like the pen of a ready writer*
> *And what the Father gives to me I'll sing*
> *I only want to be His breath I only want to glorify the King.*

Those words were beginning to be fulfilled.

# FOUR

# BELFAST CHRISTIAN FAMILY

## CITY O CITY

The Lord was teaching us a lot about being committed to each other as the Christians were in the Book of Acts and about living in community and sharing together.

At that time a number of men I had met on my travels in England began to visit us and share what God was doing in their situations. Men like John Noble, Maurice Smith, and Gerald Coates. We found that the Lord was teaching us the same kinds of things about 'church' as He had been teaching them for some years, things like, 'body ministry' where every member of the Body of Christ has gifts and anointing from God for the building up of His Body the church, not just one pastor doing everything as we had been familiar with in our previous churches. We also learnt about the ministry gifts to the church, people who were called and anointed as apostles, prophets, pastors, teachers and evangelists.

Worship was innovative and exciting as many new songs were written and learned from across the world, and we moved away from singing only traditional hymns. We enjoyed prophetic worship in dance and drama and people expressed their worship through art and craft.

There were prophecies and words of knowledge in our meetings and the Lord gave people prophetic pictures. I began to share the principles that God was teaching me from the Bible. We had a lovely growing flourishing house church. That was about to change!

On one of my visits to England I went to a meeting at Pip and J's church in Bristol. Pip and J's was St. Phillip and St James Anglican Church and they were experiencing the move of the Holy Spirit. Arthur Wallis was speaking. Arthur was one of the house church leaders I had met on my first visit to England. He was an amazing preacher and though he never got excited, what he said was exciting. That day I heard him say,

> *'Find out what God is doing in your generation and do it with all your heart.'*

I thought that was good advice. 'I am going home to Belfast and I am going to do some serious praying because I had always been a serious young man, so I prayed and prayed, for I wanted to know what God was doing. I knew what He was doing really, He was doing what I was doing, wasn't He? He was building the first house church in Ireland, I mean. Come on! 'Lord just tell me. Re-affirm me here. You're doing what I'm doing. You know it and I know it but it would be nice to just hear it again.'

So I prayed and I said, 'Lord what are You doing in my city and in my generation?'
The answer came, 'David, right now I'm baptising Roman Catholics in the Holy Spirit.'

I don't suppose reading this that you are very shocked by that. I certainly was at that time. I was brought up a Protestant, an evangelical fundamentalist. The definition of a fundamentalist is mostly mental and not much fun. That's what I was. I knew the Bible inside out and still read it inside out and I knew that a Catholic couldn't be a Christian. Or if they were a Christian they would leave the Catholic Church and come and join my church. I knew that.

I was wrong but I didn't know I was wrong; it was all I knew; so when God said 'I'm baptising Roman Catholics in the Holy Spirit' I wasn't very happy. I was in a dilemma. On the one hand I wanted to do what God was doing but on the other hand He was baptising Roman Catholics in the Holy Spirit.

So I said to the Lord. 'I don't like that' Then He said 'All right, we'll write that in God's book, David Matthews doesn't like what God is doing. Now are you satisfied?'

I thought I'd better think of something quick. 'No I'm not, I don't agree with it! You know as well as I know that Catholics can't be Christians.'

'Okay, I will write that in the book. David Matthews does not agree with what God Almighty is doing. Now are you satisfied? I didn't ask you to like what I was doing, I didn't ask you to agree with it, I just asked you to do it.' Then I said 'Lord what do you want me to do?'

Once again He took me into the Bible and I saw from the book of Acts where Peter went to the house of the Gentile Cornelius that he said,

*'The Holy Spirit came on them as He had on us at the beginning.'*

So if God gave them the same gift as He gave us who believe on the Lord Jesus Christ, who was I to think that I could oppose God?'

I had a lot of re-thinking to do and a lot of praying. I did not want to find myself in the place where I was opposing God. Now God was asking me to 'cross the divide' between Protestants and Roman Catholics. Deep down in my heart I knew that I was part of the problem in Northern Ireland with my distrust of Catholics and my prejudices; and now I said 'Lord, I don't want to be part of the problem any more, I want to be part of the solution.'

And so we began to bring the two sides together and also we were helping to give a kick-start to Catholic Charismatic Renewal in Ireland.

I had come in contact with a young man called Des Dick who led a Catholic Charismatic Prayer Group in West Belfast, a Republican area. Our groups met together with others at the chaplaincy church at Queens University in Belfast. We got to know each other a bit and decided that as Protestants and Catholics we would continue to get together in ecumenical Charismatic meetings.

I was still conflicted and my conflict was growing because I met these people who obviously loved Jesus more than I did and they were still Catholic and not only that, but happily Catholic. They weren't at all bothered about being Catholic, they weren't even questioning it. But we all knew Jesus and were baptised in the Holy Spirit.

Holy nuns attended these meetings as well as priests and laity. One of the nuns had a vision one night; she called it a picture. Protestants tended to call these things visions and when the Protestants prophesied they said, 'thus says the Lord.' But the Catholics said 'yea my people'.

And this sister had a 'picture' and she saw a jellyfish with a dagger in its back. My Catholic friends looked down the row at me because I was supposed to cover these things and provide an interpretation. Now, to this day I don't know what that meant!

One of the main characteristics of Catholic Renewal in Ireland was the 'charismatic prayer group.' These had sprung up all over the place. Des Dick led one of these prayer groups in a strong Republican area across the city in West Belfast. God quickly brought us together as an ecumenical community, two thirds Protestant and one third Roman Catholic and we became 'Belfast Christian Family'.

We learnt from the anti-segregationists in the States. We thought if we have home groups they will either be all Protestant or all Roman Catholic because we lived in sectarian ghettos, so we decided to mix the groups by bussing people across the city, as they did in America.

If we were going to a home group or a leaders' meeting in West Belfast, which was IRA territory, then they would send a car for us. People who knew the area drove us in and they said, 'If we are stopped let us do the talking.'

One night we were in Des Dick's house in West Belfast having a leaders' meeting and suddenly I saw the two men sitting near the window dive to the floor. I thought, 'Has the Holy Spirit fallen on them?

Then I heard the gunfire. When you hear gunfire you don't have to wait to decide if you should fall over. You just fall. And what I didn't know but they could see, was that there was an IRA sniper in the garden shooting at British soldiers down the street and they were returning fire. Blessed are the peacemakers.

As we enjoyed fellowship we began to explore ways that our two groups could meet more regularly. We found that the secret was to emphasise the truths and practices that united us and agree to differ about the others. Some of these things were political as well as scriptural.

One of the biggest ones was the Mass (Communion). So the sixty or so people from a Protestant background continued to break bread together, in our traditional way, while our thirty or so

Catholic brothers and sisters continued to attend Mass and observe their obligations to their church. We all met together on Sunday in a local community centre and in small groups throughout the week.

When the leaders had meetings together, they often came home late as they had to wait until it was safe to travel across the city. There were a lot of prayers for their protection in those days. They were literally in danger of their lives.

We shared together in our weddings, infant baptisms, infant dedications, adult baptisms and even a few funerals. We shared picnics, lunches, and holiday conferences together and over a period of time as couples in the community married some of them bought houses in or near Ladas Drive where Mary and I lived. Gary and Alice had a house directly behind ours, with a hole in the hedge which we used frequently. Andy and Barbara lived round the corner and Nigel and Heather later moved in next door.

Our good friends Cathy and Des Dick were married. It was the first time I had been at a Roman Catholic wedding. The Catholic Church felt strange with the statues, crucifixes, and The Stations of the Cross. I discovered a lot of things about Catholicism that I had not known before. For example, we always believed that Catholics had the crucifix in the central place because they did not believe that Jesus had risen from the dead, but that he was still on the cross.

My Catholic friend told me that they always believed that we had the empty cross as our symbol because we believed it was the cross that saved us and not the man on the cross.

I also became aware of just how much prejudice and discrimination there had been against Catholics in Northern Ireland and we had discussions about law and order. One of our friends said:

'Law and Order is all very well, but what if the law excludes you and the order discriminates against you?' I really was having my understanding of the society I lived in widened. Later on, our group Belfast Christian Family organised some big gatherings in the centre of Belfast. We listened to Roman Catholic Charismatic Renewal speakers such as Ralph Martin and Steve Clarke and Francis McNutt from the States and enjoyed lively spirit-led worship.

We could have said, 'Baa Baa black sheep' and God would still have anointed it because 'where brothers dwell together in unity there I have commanded the blessing!'

I'll never forget hugging my first nun. I wasn't sure how to do it appropriately but it was wonderful. And in came the Paisleyites. We were vilified by Ian Paisley. I thought we must be doing something right and they came in to the meetings with their big Bibles and their suits and ties on. They came to spy us out.

They were sitting behind a nun. I thought this will be fun. We were worshipping the Lord singing in tongues and lifting our hands and the nun, bless her, was right in it. I could see that these Paisleyites were getting more and more agitated. One of them tapped her on the shoulder and said belligerently, 'What about Mary then?' To which the nun replied,'Oh thank you, I'd forgotten about Our Lady. Hail Mary full of Grace, the Lord is with thee. Blessed art thou among women...' They weren't impressed.

In that same meeting I looked at the back and a young British soldier had come in dressed in full battle dress with his gun because they were patrolling the streets of Belfast to stop us from killing each other. I don't know what brought him in, maybe he had heard the singing, maybe he was a Christian, I don't know, but in he came. And a nun walked up to him, put her arms round him and hugged him.

*David' story continues at Chapter 11*
*after some testimonies from those*
*who were part of his story...*
*... at the beginning*

# FIVE

# DES DICK'S STORY

We had a Catholic Charismatic prayer group on the Falls Road in Belfast which grew from about a dozen people in the early seventies until in 1975 there were between 200 and 250 people coming each week. Those of us who were leading the group had quite busy lives with prayer meetings, seminars, leader's weekends and lots more but we felt that our personal relationship with God was being lost in the midst of all the activity,

So in 1976 I went to visit the Ann Arbor Community in America. They were a group who had been involved in Charismatic Renewal from the beginning in the late sixties. I was impressed by the standard of spirituality in the community as I saw how they had taken the experience of Baptism in the Spirit and the power it had released in people's lives and channelled it into personal holiness and committed relationships. It wasn't chaotic and disorganised like a lot of charismatic groups where people are experience, gift, or ministry orientated. They had built a community of a thousand people who loved one another and shared their quality of life together. I was so impressed by the quality of their life together.

I came back home and thought, 'well that's something of what we need'. I called together the core group from the prayer meeting, the 20 or 30 we had been meeting with the longest, and together we began to work out relationships and commitment to each other. That was the start of a Catholic Community growing on the Falls Road.

I met David Matthews and we met up with each other quite a lot in those days. Both of us were in a group of charismatic leaders called the 'Northern Service Committee' so we had a great deal of contact with each other. I was impressed with David because of his no-nonsense approach to things. A lot of strange things went on in the Charismatic Renewal, peculiar prophecy, speaking out in tongues without interpretation and that kind of thing. He was one of the few people I heard saying it was crazy. Everybody was so spiritual, all you had to do was say 'thus says the Lord' and no-one would dare question or challenge it. David did, and that impressed me. There was an element of reality about him.

David and I just got on very well together and as we talked more and more about our respective groups we saw that in building relationships and commitment within our separate groups (as they were also already doing in Ravenhill Park) we were essentially the same kind of thing. And so we began to do some things together, mainly men's meetings and week-ends together, that sort of thing. We had a lot of fun together as well. At a men's retreat in a convent one of my lovely protestant brothers borrowed a statue of Our Lady and put it in my bed. I was unmarried at the time. What sacrilege. I don't think the holy sisters were too scandalised.

We began to feel that each group could support the other in what they were doing. I don't think either of us had any idea that we would come together in the way we did; it certainly wasn't planned that way at the beginning. However at one of the men's meetings we had together God clearly spoke to us about 'coming together to be one people.' So we took His word seriously and started to work it out.

The initial reaction from the protestant group would have been incredible fear and suspicion of the other side and I think some would have preferred ignorant fear rather than the reality of pursuing unity. It required a new way of thinking about other people who now were clearly the Lord's. We all had to start from the fact that we were brothers and sisters in Christ rather than, 'How much does this brother agree with me in terms of doctrine'. We had to talk through all sorts of issues and were surprised by the number of basics we agreed on.

On the Catholic side, to be honest nobody was really that excited about it at the time, in fact I think we would all have been quite happy if the Lord hadn't said it. We were willing to co-operate at a superficial level but the Lord had clearly told us that the two original groups would have to die and that He would build a new thing. Not everybody on both sides appreciated that. We were in the middle of a civil war and felt that people would despise it and think us traitors to our own side! What we were doing was actually dangerous.

We found that for us the biggest problems weren't doctrinal or theological; the real issues were fear and suspicion. We had been brought up and educated in two different camps, literally, in East and West Belfast. If you said something the other person would wonder 'Is he saying something else, or is he implying this or that?' It took us a long time to get over that.

Even travelling into opposite sides of the city was scary. I never knew East Belfast; it might as well have been Birmingham. I didn't know the roads or the streets and I had to start travelling there to meet people. It was like driving into enemy territory.

We had a system of 'social' or 'spiritual' bussing. We weren't likely to just drop in on someone across the divide, so we had a system of small groups which met weekly and people swapped groups every month or so. It was just a means of getting to know people from the opposite side.

I think this helped us to overcome barriers; we met people in their homes discovered the same human condition, needs and insecurities as ourselves, and in seeing 'the others' love for the Lord we realised that a lot of our fears and suspicions were unfounded.

# SIX

# DAVID PRESTON'S STORY

Baptism in the Spirit? I have always wondered when it actually happened! I spoke in tongues when I was about 15 years old on a foreign missions trip to the South of Ireland – they were all foreigners down there and especially needy since they were Catholics! Every evangelical 'knew' that you could not be a Christian and a Catholic! No marks for bias. But I don't know that I would call that experience of speaking in tongues as my baptism in the Spirit and I know that will offend some people's theology right there.

What I do know was that I had a very sensitive conscience and the devil was giving me merry hell in reminding me of all the things I did or thought, that were not up to the standard. And living up to the standard was how I viewed the ways things were supposed to be. I had stolen money from my parents when I was about ten years old and I was being reminded now that I had never apologised even though I was caught and duly 'dealt with'. A battle raged within me as to whether I should go and apologise. The inner condemnation was high and life was miserable. The killer punch was of course that if I was not prepared to make the apology even at the expense of severe humiliation, then I was obviously not surrendered to God where it mattered. Those were the thoughts that raged within me.

The conviction of course was not from God, but I did not know that at the time, I finally decided in the quietness of my room that I would pay the price and go and seek forgiveness from my parents. They were of course oblivious to the inner turmoil going on within me and would have been surprised that an issue of some nine or ten years ago was even in my mind. No sooner had I decided to act than a peace came into my heart and a flood of joy as I realised that Jesus had died so that I did not have to climb any steps through to Jesus the door. He was the door and it was on ground level! There was no need to make these humiliating confessions.

I could give this testimony and many would consider it as my conversion to Christ, even though I had a made a profession at the age of ten, but to me this was the entrance to the life of the Spirit. It doesn't fit the model as baptism in the Spirit, but I am sure God is not concerned to fit any model. Theologically, for me, baptism in the Spirit is my being joined to Christ, not the anointing of the Spirit upon me or the speaking in tongues, and I have known all three.

Once in the realm of the Spirit, it was natural to want to be with and meet those of like mind. I met for several years with like-minded believers in Queen's University and we prayed together for several hours every day. I met my wife, Janet, while on Operation Mobilisation and our initial conversations were avid expositions of the book of Romans! At a fellowship meeting in Scotland we heard of a similar gathering in Northern Ireland and on my return to Belfast, we eagerly sought out David Matthews, who I later found had attended the same school as I had – only a year or two above me. We met for quite some time in Carrickfergus before David felt a call to Belfast and the venue of our meetings became the name of the Fellowship – Ravenhill Park. I lived with David and Mary for several months before my wedding in Birmingham. On the first day of my stay, Mary got up to make my breakfast, but I was too cheerful at that time of the morning and Mary decided I did not need any help to get out for work. It was the first and last prepared breakfast for me at no 83.

Those were heady days as the group slowly grew to some 50 in number. I remember my first prophecy – 'speak to me the things that are true'. It probably meant very little to others at the time but for me it was the declaration that truth was not embodied in how I felt at any one time. We found out that a small group of believers were meeting some 100 metres from where we lived and we joined forces together. We were introduced to the wider group of English Leaders – John Noble, Gerald Coates, Maurice Smith and had weekends together with titles like 'Just for Joy' as the reason for meeting. There were the charismatic meetings in the City Centre and the gradual recognition that Catholics, too, were enjoying a life in the Spirit and were therefore our brothers and sisters. A certain Desmond Dick featured as one of the leaders of the Ladybrook Fellowship and Derek Poole in Portadown. We met for a day of prayer together and one after another the prophetic word was for the Catholics to meet as one. Shortly after we became one group.

This was a lonely path for David. He carried the responsibility for doing something that no one else was doing. Even amongst those in England with whom he was closely associated, there was some doubt as to the wisdom of what he was doing, or even whether God was behind it at all! There was a lot of talk about what name to call ourselves, but we settled for Belfast Christian Family – largely through David's influence. In fact, if the truth were told, most of what we did was because of David's influence and leadership. Nowhere in Northern Ireland in the midst of the troubles was any group modelling Catholic and Protestant together. We loved being together and booked a weekend together in Castlewellan Castle to meet, to eat, and to be around each other. The Landlord didn't quite match our joy and admonished us for – of all things - using too much toilet paper. We were a young group with small children – what did they expect!

We determined that the early days would include no discussions on doctrine, but we would take the time to get to know each other. We would travel over to Ladybrook Avenue, a very catholic area, and praise and worship together. The Catholics would come across to Ravenhill, past the 'big man's church (Rev Ian K Paisley Senior) in fear and trepidation. Everyone checked to see if their car doors were locked while travelling. It was a battle to overcome fear.

My early memories were of travelling to the Catholic areas to run small Bible studies. It was the time of the hunger strikes and sometimes by the time I had finished the study, another hunger striker had died and the roads were filled with burning buses. I practised my Irish accent with a godly fervency in case anyone stopped the car. I already knew that the shibboleth of the Northern Counties was pronouncing the letter 'H' with an aspirate. No use pretending to be Catholic if you pronounced 'hospital' with a 'normal' H. You were probably going to be going directly to the hospital anyway if you did that, with only a few broken bones if you were lucky. Cars were hijacked and left with bombs inside to kill police. So the police stopped checking cars and you had to check your own if it was stolen. Dorothy, a slightly older girl in the Fellowship had her car stolen and I was the 'lucky' one, as one of the leaders in BCF, to go and collect it. There it was on the top of a hill, the area cordoned off and the police some 100 metres from the car. It was a lonely walk to the car. I mean – what does a novice check for? Wires coming out of the ignition, a bomb visible inside the car? The IRA were too clever for that. I swallowed hard, said a quick prayer – more like 'Oh God Help!' and opened the door. And here I am today penning these words in memory.

I remember the first meeting we had in a Catholic area and Des Dick boldly declaring that this ground was not Catholic ground or Protestant territory. It was God's place because we were there as children of God. We had house groups and worship meetings and the whole experience was alive as we met with God, sang our hearts out in worship and often listened to David speaking and the words touched our hearts rather than feed our minds. There was discipline as well. I remember David telling me to put away my concordance. That I often answered questions from the Bible that no one was asking! This was good advice. It made me concentrate on hearing the voice of God in prophecy and enabled me to put the teaching gift to the side. In the early days, the gift was so covered over in inessentials that it would have been hard to see it as a gift at all!

I think apart from the thrill of following the Spirit, there was the very strong sense of belonging and sharing and generosity. Why buy several lawnmowers, when you can borrow from your fellow believer or he/she from you. Why call in workmen when you had the willing help from members of the fellowship? And when a need became known, we all chipped in generously to meet it. Issues were talked about, disagreements sorted and there was a very strong sense of unity and belonging. Being in BCF gave us a strong sense of love and identity; it was like coming home. It was every bit a church, but so so different from anything on offer elsewhere.

*David Preston, 2017*

# SEVEN

# JANET PRESTON
# WORSHIP IN DANCE

I received the Holy Spirit as a young person when, as a Protestant evangelical, I was 'born again'. I have always loved dance since as long as I can remember and so I was thrilled to enter college at the age of eighteen and take up dance as part of my Physical Education Teacher Training.

After my marriage to my husband David Preston in 1974, I moved from England to his home city of Belfast in Northern Ireland and became part of a small house church called Ravenhill Park Fellowship led by David Matthews. It was here I learned to worship in spontaneously creative ways responding to the prophetic word that, 'He wanted us to take risks in His kingdom'.

The Holy Spirit seemed to use the very thing that I loved doing, to express my love for Him, and that was dance. During this time, I also had the joy and privilege of dancing on the beach after a fellowship baptism in the sea of some friends. The theme was a declaration, 'whatsoever you bind on earth it shall be bound in Heaven and whatsoever you loose, will be made free'.

It seemed that music and movement were coming together to remind us of God's promises. One of the songs that I loved to move to was written by Ronnie Wilson a member of our fellowship:

> 'I hear the sound of rustling in the leaves of the trees.
> The Spirit of the Lord has come down on the earth.'

It echoed exactly what was happening at that time as God's Spirit was moving across all denominations. After this, several church members asked me to teach them how to worship using dance. We began to use the worship songs that were being created at that time interpreting the lyrics. We had a lot of fun creating set dances together, letting go of our inhibitions, getting in touch with our emotions whilst learning to locate the Spirit of God in each one of us as we worshipped God in a brand new way. I have a vivid memory of attending a conference at Castlewellan Castle when I was nine months pregnant and setting aside all inhibition to dance, 'Just for Joy' – the reason for our coming together.

What God was doing by His Spirit amongst all the people of God came to our attention as we were invited to use our dances in worship in other gatherings; at a Presbyterian women's conference first and then at a much larger ecumenical gathering in the centre of Belfast City. At this large gathering there were people of all denominations enjoying a fresh outpouring of the Holy Spirit and as we danced out the Creation Story, the joy was tangible.

In keeping with what was happening at that time the Lord spoke to two very different groups of people – a Catholic Charismatic prayer group from West Belfast and our House Church from East Belfast - asking them to come together as one. Hence Belfast Christian Family was birthed and it was during this time that men and women from both backgrounds came together to produce a dance that portrayed the fact that a single cell cannot survive alone.

The Holy Spirit was seeking to remind us of our need for each other and of how the extension of His Kingdom would be accomplished. It was very humbling and at the same time rewarding to work together – men and women, Catholic and Protestant – allowing Dance to unite us in our desire to worship Him. We developed lasting friendships at a time when there was much conflict and suspicion raging outside in the City. The Spirit of God enabled us to be a witness amid such hatred and sectarianism.

As I look back to the beginning of the Charismatic movement I thank God for the freedom He released in me to worship Him through dance, to open the way for others and to enable us to express unity in the Body of Christ as we created dance together. And the blessing continues to this day, albeit in the sub-continent of India where David and I in our 'retirement' now work as missionaries.

*Janet Preston, 2017*

# EIGHT

# PAT COLLINS, C.M.
# THAT THEY ALL MAY BE ONE

I grew up as the Counter-Reformation in the Catholic Church was coming to an end. It had held sway from the end of the Council of Trent in 1563 to the announcement of the second Vatican Council in 1959. I can remember my mother telling me about it when I was 14. When I asked her what the Council aimed to do, she said, 'I think it is going to try to heal the rift between the Catholic and Protestant Churches.' She wasn't far wrong. In 1964 the Decree on Ecumenism began with these words, 'The restoration of unity among all Christians is one of the principal concerns of the Second Vatican Council.... division openly contradicts the will of Christ, scandalises the world, and damages the holy cause of preaching the Gospel to every creature.'

I think that the connection between inter-church unity and effective evangelisation is a vital one. The extent to which unity is lacking in and between churches is the extent to which their evangelisation will lack credibility and effectiveness.

When I was ordained a few years after the ending of the Council, I was sent to St Patrick's College in Armagh. The troubles were at their height in Northern Ireland. During the next three years I felt a growing spiritual unease within that context of violence. I knew something was missing in my life, but couldn't put my finger on what it was.

On Feb 4th 1974 I heard Rev Cecil Kerr speaking about the fact that Jesus is our peace and how he breaks down the dividing wall between Jews and Gentiles, Catholics and Protestants. Quite frankly, his inspired words moved me to tears. I wanted to know the Lord the way Cecil already did. I told him that I was looking for a new awareness of God in my life. He read a memorable passage from Eph 3:16-20. Then he began to pray over me, firstly in English, then in tongues. Suddenly, and effortlessly, I too began to pray fluently in tongues. I knew with great conviction that Jesus loved me and accepted me as I was. As a result of that religious awakening, I was fully persuaded that the Lord was strongly at work in members of other churches.

Afterwards Cecil and I became great friends. He used to say that there would be no genuine reconciliation without renewal in the Holy Spirit, and no genuine renewal in the Holy Spirit without reconciliation. Over the years I witnessed the fact that once Catholics and Protestants were baptised in the Holy Spirit they had a God prompted desire to work for inter-church reconciliation and to carry out the great commission by evangelising separately and together. In the mid 1970s a number of people who had been baptised in the Holy Spirit formed the Northern Ireland Service Committee.

It was made up of male and female members of many Churches.

We leaders often met, usually in the Christian Renewal Centre in Rostrevor. There we would pray, discern and plan together. For example, we ran a Northern Ireland Charismatic Conference each year. One of the most memorable was one which took place in Church House in Belfast during the general strike of May 1974. It was a wonderful festival of praise, during which we received a prophecy which said that 'the work and the weapons are one, they are praise... praise is the shortcut to holiness.' Ps 89:15 says, 'Blessed are the people who know the festal shout.' During that inter church festival we received an anointing that enabled us to know that God was living in the united praises of his people while having prophetic intimations that peace would eventually come.

I can recall another occasion when a number of Catholics and Protestants were invited to conduct a day of renewal in Larne in Northern Ireland. David McKee, a Presbyterian minister gave the talks. Afterwards he asked Larry Kelly, a Catholic lay man, Harry Woodhead, an Anglican vicar, and myself to join him in praying for people. As we did so, many of them, Catholics and Protestants alike, began to fall to the ground under the power of the Holy Spirit. When the meeting was over, David called me aside. 'That is the first time I have ever seen people resting in the Spirit' he said, 'why do you think it has happened?' 'As far as I'm concerned,' I replied, 'There can be only one answer. God is honouring our united witness, by blessing our ministry in a special way. As Ps 133 says: 'How good and delightful it is to live together as brothers and sisters for there Yahweh bestows a blessing.'

I remember another time when a number of leaders from different Churches met in Rostrevor. During the prayer time I saw in my mind's eye a number of tall flagpoles with their respective flags flapping in the wind. At the base of each were groups of people. They were shouting and gesticulating in an angry way at the men and women gathered around the other flagpoles. After a time I noticed the cross of Calvary in the middle of the surrounding circle of flagpoles. At first, the protesting people didn't even notice it. But as they did, one by one the belligerent men and women began to be aware of the crucified Lord. Then each one of the groups began to lower its flag, some slowly, others more rapidly. Soon the cross stood higher than all the flags. People began to drift away from their flagpoles to gather around the foot of the cross. Then I heard the Lord say,

> *'At the moment the flags of your denominational and nationalistic pride are raised higher than the cross. But when you look to me who was lifted up from the earth to draw all people to myself, you will lower the flags of your pride. Then and only then, will you find peace, for in the power of my cross the dividing walls of your divisions will crumble.'*

Not surprisingly, that vision was an inspiration not only to me but to those with whom I shared it, in our work for reconciliation. In 1990 Rev. Cecil Kerr included it in his book, *The Way of Peace*.

During the 70s I can remember meeting American writer and speaker, Steve Clark, in the Europa Hotel in Belfast at a time when he was a speaker at one of our Northern conferences. In the course of conversation he spoke about an ancient king whose baby son was captured during a war and subsequently raised as the son of the enemy king. In adult life he went into battle with what used to be his native tribe and killed his father. He rejoiced to have killed the enemy king, not knowing he was in fact guilty of patricide. Then Clark observed, 'His problem was one that is common in Northern Ireland, it is a problem of recognition. Like that young soldier Catholics and Protestant often fail to acknowledge that their so called enemies are in fact their brothers and sisters, children of their heavenly Father.'

I also met David Matthews, my brother in the Lord, in the mid 70s. He was leading a house church in Belfast at that time, which later became an ecumenical community, Belfast Christian Family. I admired the fact that he was devoid of prejudice, understood Catholics and could relate to them with ease. I can recall one occasion when we ministered together at the Chaplaincy in Queens University in Belfast. Cecil Kerr was the Chaplain there at that time. David gave a talk during which he quoted the words, 'where your treasure is, there your heart will be also' (Mt 6:21). Then he asked, 'what is your treasure?' to which he offered a memorable reply, 'It is whatever you think about most.'

Later we held a healing service together and I can recall getting a word of knowledge about a woman who was suffering from a scary recurrence of breast cancer. A Protestant nurse was present who was suffering from that very complaint. We prayed for her. Many years later I met her in Lurgan and she told me that she had been healed. Subsequently, David moved to England and I only met him occasionally at conferences.

In recent years we bumped into one another in Birmingham when we were both staying with a barrister and his wife. While there, David told me about his unexpected intention of becoming a Catholic. Then he proceeded to ask me to hear his confession in accord with the teaching of James 5:16. It was one of the most humbling and moving moments I have ever experienced. Subsequently, David, his wife Mary and daughter took the conscientious step of being received into the Catholic Church. Since then, we have continued to be impelled by the words of Jesus, 'that they all may be one' (John 17:21). In spite of David's struggle with illness we have had the joy of speaking together at conferences in St Andrews and Southport.

I want to end with some words that Pope John Paul II wrote in par. 54 of The Church in Europe (2003), because they express what I learned, especially during the precious time I spent in Northern Ireland 'The task of evangelisation involves moving toward one another and moving forward together as Christians ...evangelisation and unity, evangelisation and ecumenism are indissolubly linked.'

*Pat Collins CM, 2017*

# NINE

# A GOD OF SURPRISES
# JOHN NOBLE

Our God is full of surprises! How did John Noble, the guy who wrote that little pamphlet 'Forgive Us Our Denominations', which was so unwelcome among Christian leaders at the time, become so deeply involved with the Roman Catholic renewal?

Clive Calver, a key leader at Spring Harvest here in the UK, made the point that the historic divisions among Christians which had been vertical as we hid within our church structures, were being brushed aside as the Holy Spirit was poured out in Renewal during the 1960's. He went on to say that the divisions were increasingly becoming horizontal, as those receiving the Spirit found one another across the streams and those opposed to the Renewal found a measure of unity in their opposition.

Well, as the author of the pamphlet, I believe I was misunderstood. My problem was not with the many devout Christians in the denominations but rather with the 'ism' of those who believed that they alone were the guardians of truth. Indeed, I pointed out that the worst brand of 'ism' was the 'I am of Christ' company, proud of their non-alignment.

As I journeyed with the Holy Spirit, in what came to be known as the House Church Movement, I discovered that many evangelicals who I felt closest to in doctrine as being right, were 'dead' right, with the emphasis on dead! However, in Renewal, I met Catholics, who thought very differently to me, yet were clearly filled with the Spirit of grace and open to see Jesus in others who were very different to them.

Many who we were closest to withdrew from fellowship as we began to meet in homes and even pubs. On the other hand, our Catholic friends were not at all 'phased' by this and certainly didn't seem to have a problem with the pub as a venue. Indeed, whilst we were at the other end of the Charismatic spectrum, they seemed quite secure to trust their discernment and share with us in an ever deepening friendship.

This was expressed in a remarkable way in the 1970's as the Lord connected us with Dave and Mary Matthews in Belfast where they were growing a community under the name of 'The Belfast Christian Family'. There, in the midst of 'The Troubles', they were bucking the trend of hatred and division by bringing together a motley crew of young people touched by the Holy Spirit from Catholic and non-Catholic backgrounds.

What times we had! Fun, friendship and appreciation released a Spirit of creativity in worship and new songs flowed out in torrents and a beautiful stream carried them all around the world.

During my numerous visits I came to appreciate their boldness as they moved on to one another's territory to make new friends and to minister to others. There was a genuine Spirit of unity which was not dependent on agreeing about everything but was based on a willingness to listen and remain open to the Spirit.

I remember a conversation I had with Des Dick, one of the young Catholic leaders, as we shared our understanding of church. After discussion Des made it clear that he believed that eventually I would join the Catholic Church. 'How could that be?' I asked. 'Wait and see,' he said, 'we Catholics will change so much as we embrace the renewal you will be able to take that step!' 'Well,' said I, 'I can live with that Des.'

The fact is that some of our friends have taken that step, not least among them David and Mary Matthews and, a relatively new friend, Ulf Ekman, a respected church leader in Sweden.

Many will remember 1974 when Jimmy and Carol Owens timely musical 'Come Together' took the UK by storm. Groups all over the country did 'come together' to sing, worship and pray demonstrating our hunger for greater unity among Christians. It was a special time and we took performances to 13 centres!

At our final event as we were preparing to leave, one of our song writers, Bob Gillman, said, 'I've written a new song.' It was late and reluctantly we gave him a hearing. He picked up his guitar and began to sing 'Bind us together, Lord, bind us together, with cords that cannot be broken...' We were not hugely impressed but we recognised that this was a prophetic cry, a prayer from the heart and, well, the rest is history!

That song went all over the world. Still today, forty years on, it is stirring hearts as the Spirit yearns and moves through God's people to bring fulfilment to Jesus' prayer. Friends travelling in the Himalayas heard the strains coming from mud huts and Pope John Paul sang it with hundreds of thousands of pilgrims in St Peter's Square in Rome!

In 1979 and 1980, together with Gerald Coates, we took the 'Bind Us Together' tour to cities in the UK, to Dublin and Scandinavia. We have many happy memories of that amazing time but one of the enduring highlights was the meeting in Belfast's Ulster Hall: The hall was packed with Christians from all backgrounds, including a great throng of Catholic nuns in their habits praising Jesus with hands raised in adoration. In the midst of those dark days in the province the Holy Spirit was working and brought his people together in a great demonstration of love and unity. Thank you so much Dave, Mary, and BCF for hosting that wonderful evening.

On reflection, we must have done something right as we were picketed outside the entrance of the hall. On the one hand, Paisleyites claimed we were undercover Catholics seeking to infiltrate the Protestant churches; on the other hand, fervent Catholic activists accused us of trying to get their people to leave the Catholic Church. Inside the hall we were all just enjoying Jesus and loving one another to bits!

In 1984 I was elected Chairman of the National Charismatic Leaders Conference founded by my long time friend Michael Harper. (He had helped Christine and me on our journey to faith when he was working out of All Souls as Chaplain to the Oxford Street Stores.) By this time I was leading a network of House Churches and, as such, was very involved in the Renewal.

At this particular conference a keen young Catholic leader was finding his way around the maze of relationships that were developing across the streams. Gerald Coates and I recognised the huge potential in this young man and invited him to join us at some of our leaders' gatherings which he, Charles Whitehead, gladly accepted. Thus began one of the key links which enabled us to work more closely alongside the Catholic Renewal, not only in the UK, but also around the world.

About this time we started meetings at the Westminster Central Hall with our new found Catholic friends. They were specially designed to bring House Church Christians and renewed Catholics together for teaching, prayer and worship. Right from the start those meetings were heaving with expectant worshippers who came into an atmosphere of faith and the Lord did not disappoint.

There was no concern that we differed in our understanding of many aspects of theology. We were all simply thrilled to be together and discover that we all partook of the same Holy Spirit and loved the same Jesus. Our differences could be shared in other forums against this background of love and acceptance.

Creativity in worship was a hallmark as prophetic movement accompanied scripture reading, drama, dance and 'movement in worship' by a young man called Andy Au enhanced ministry and new worship songs abounded. Those ministering, be they towering giants of the Renewal, like Cardinal Leo Joseph Suenans or plain old Dave Matthews, were received with equal enthusiasm.

Of course, we were naive and made mistakes but there was a spirit of generosity. In one pre-meeting run-through of the programme one Catholic Priest said, 'after prayers we'll have Kyrie Eleison.' One of our number immediately responded, 'Oh, great! But why does she have to sing three times?'

From the connections with Charles and Michael Harper, I was drawn into the planning of two major international conferences. Michael had, what turned out to be, a divine appointment at an international airport when he and Larry Christensen, a Lutheran Charismatic Leader, and Father Tom Forrest met and shared a cup of tea. From what appeared to be a chance meeting two great conferences emerged.

Berne 1990 was a European-wide gathering hosted by Martin Buehlmann, an independent Charismatic leader and Marcel Dietler, a Lutheran pastor both with churches in the city. It was God's timing as the Berlin wall came down enabling hundreds of Eastern Europeans Christians Catholics and Protestants to join us. Significantly the conference theme was 'Hope for Europe' and our own Andy Au, dancing with banners, led a great 'March for Jesus' praise event through the town.

Again Catholics, House Church Christians and many other denominations from all over Europe, were demonstrating that the Holy Spirit is a spirit of unity and grace. It was clear that this same Holy Spirit was preparing his people to take up their high calling to be Good News, and to take Good News to every corner of our great continent.

Brighton 1991 quickly followed and it was another giant step, bringing 5,000 Christian leaders from every continent together to share, pray and consider the great commission to reach all peoples with the Gospel in the power of the Holy Spirit. It was here that many of us first met Father Raniero Cantalamessa, preacher to the Papal Household, who ministered alongside Archbishop George Carey and Cardinal Basil Hume. He was a lovely gentle man who became a real friend of the Renewal here in the UK.

There was also great excitement as we were joined by church leaders who were actually experiencing revival in many areas of the world. Apart from the incredible stories of outpourings, of miracles and hearing of multitudes coming to Jesus, new bonds of friendship were forged which remain to this day. I can testify to receiving ministry from those we met at that conference and as a result, I travelled thousands of miles to share with and serve those new found friends.

It was wonderful to see Catholics and Pentecostals from areas where there was considerable disharmony, competition and even persecution, beginning to fellowship together as barriers came down. What a privilege to be a part of all the Lord was doing in those great gatherings. Their influence is still being felt as unity among Charismatic Christian continues to grow and move the purposes of God forward in greater co-operation in mission around the world.

Finally, I can't close without mentioning the 'Gathering in the Holy Spirit' meetings which have been taking place in Rome for some years. Hosted by Father Jim Puglisi director of the Centro Pro Unione, they have drawn Charismatic Catholic and non-denominational leaders from Europe and the USA together for fellowship, prayer and discussion. The idea developed from the many other international leadership forums too numerous to refer to here. The purpose was to further understanding between these two groupings which were becoming more influential in mission and social action around the world.

They proved to be a tremendous blessing with the highlight

being a visit with the Pontifical Council for the Promotion of Christian Unity every time we met. Eventually it was decided that 'Preliminary Conversations' between the PCPCU and a small group of non-denominational leaders would be a helpful way of increasing our appreciation of one another and might ultimately provide helpful guidelines for those working in mission together on the ground.

After struggling to help the Catholics understand who we are, our Richard Roberts wrote a brief paper in language which reached into their hearts and a light seemed to have been switched on. We are now 'thankfully, no longer referred to as 'non-denoms' but as New Charismatic Churches and this exciting journey towards unity goes on'

*John Noble, Chairman of the National Charismatic Leaders' Conference 1984 - 2006*

# TEN

# THE SURPRISES OF THE SPIRIT
# CHARLES WHITEHEAD

In February 1967, when the Holy Spirit fell on a group of American students at Duquesne University, an event which is recognised as the start of the Catholic Charismatic Renewal, Sue and I had been married for six months and were living in Bramhall, Cheshire. At that time I regarded myself as a faithful Catholic with a reasonably good understanding of doctrine and apologetics, although my attendance at church was only occasional and Sue was a committed and articulate atheist. Little did we think that this was to change dramatically nine years later in 1976, by which time we were living in Chalfont St. Peter, Buckinghamshire, and had our first two children, Lucy and Adam. So what happened to change our lives so completely?

Through the remarkable witness of a small group of Christians from different local churches – Anglican, Catholic and Baptist – I discovered that my faith was purely intellectual and was therefore of little help in my day-to-day life, whereas for them Jesus was alive and active in them all the time. I had completely failed to grasp the basic fact that the Holy Spirit, present in me through my baptism and confirmation, was there to bring me the power I needed to live an active, fulfilling and effective Christian life. But he needed my co-operation and this had been lacking. Without it, the effects of the graces I had received were very limited. Until I understood this and gave the Spirit the freedom to work in me and through me, my spiritual life was always going to be an uphill battle – one that I had very little chance of winning because we are not supposed to live the Christian life without the love and power of the Holy Spirit, although many, like me, try to do so. This is what I discovered in our small group, whilst Sue came to realise that Jesus was a living reality, not just a human invention, gave her life to him and was filled with the Holy Spirit. The Lord took her back to her Anglican roots, and as she says herself, she did not want to be an atheist on the losing side! I followed her example and opened my life to the Lord and his Holy Spirit with amazing results, and became very active in my Catholic Church.

Since then, my relationship with God is the most important thing in my life and I have been used to teach and minister in Christian churches all over the world. I spent ten years as the President of the International Catholic Charismatic Renewal Services Council (ICCRS) with an office in Vatican premises in Rome and regular access to Pope Saint John Paul II; I have written books which have been translated into a number of languages and published in different countries; I have contact with both hierarchy and laity around the world. The Lord has provided enormous opportunities for us to work ecumenically, not only with the traditional Catholic and Protestant Churches but also very much with the Pentecostal and new Independent Churches in many countries. I was the only non-Pentecostal member of the Azusa Street Centennial Cabinet in 2006, invited to contribute to the planning of the international celebration of 100 years since the birth of Pentecostalism in 1906 in Los Angeles. In this whole area of spiritual ecumenism, Pope Francis is strongly involved, based on his personal experience during his years as a Bishop and Cardinal in Buenos Aires.

It was in the 1980s that Sue and I first met David and Mary Matthews at a series of ecumenical rallies we were helping organise at Westminster Central Hall, London, with a group of Independent Church leaders. I well remember sitting next to David on the platform, looking out at a packed hall of Catholic, Protestant and Independent Church members, all alive in the Holy Spirit and worshipping God with enthusiasm and passion. David is a great preacher with an amazing knowledge of the Bible, and since that time we have worked together at a wide variety of conferences, events and meetings, bringing renewal Catholics together with charismatics from Protestant and Independent Churches in many different places. We have become very good friends with the Matthews, and so it is a great joy for me to have been asked to contribute a short chapter to this book, explaining my personal journey. Between the four of us we have experienced this renewal in the Holy Spirit from an Independent, a Protestant and a Catholic Church perspective, all made possible through our shared desire for close spiritual relationships irrespective of denomination.

Although in 1976 we had no idea what the years ahead had in store for us, we did realise that an exciting new adventure was beginning and we, like David and Mary in Northern Ireland at that time, wanted to give others the key that would start their spiritual engines too. The need to understand the person and work of the Spirit is even greater today than it was then – things have not changed for the better and we all need spiritual renewal. This had been the experience of the American students at Duquesne in 1967, and by 1976 when Sue and I became involved, the Charismatic Renewal was to be found in almost every country in the world, touching and changing the lives of millions of men and women in all nations and walks of life. No grass-roots movement in the Catholic Church had ever travelled as far, as fast or as powerfully. It was and remains unlike any other movement in Church history, for there is no inspired human founder and no common programme of formation which has to be followed. It is simply, powerfully and uniquely a loving and sovereign work of God through an outpouring of his Holy Spirit, whereby he touches individual lives in many different settings and circumstances, bringing new faith and power and setting them on fire with a love and zeal to grow in faith and to serve him and his people.

The heart of this Renewal, generally known as Baptism in the Spirit, is, as the late Cardinal Leon Josef Suenens described it,a grace of Pentecostal refreshment offered to all Christians'. As we and David and Mary very quickly discovered, it really is an ecumenical grace which has blessed people in all the Christian churches. This new life in Christ is then to be carried forth into the whole world. So this is what we are celebrating in 2017 – fifty years of a life-transforming grace poured out on the whole Catholic Church through a sovereign act of God, which started in 1967 among a group of American students. Now at last the Catholic Church had 'caught up' with what had caused the birth of Pentecostalism at Azusa Street, Los Angeles, in 1906, had been experienced in many of the traditional Protestant Churches since the 1950s, and had led to the birth of the new Independent Charismatic Churches in the 1960s and 70s.

My personal experience had been the immediate transformation of my spiritual life, resulting in a passionate desire to grow in my faith and to play my part in bringing the Good News of the saving work of Jesus to everyone. This change had nothing to do with my merits or personal abilities, but everything to do with the love, grace, mercy and power of God, freely poured out upon me. In the Oxford English Dictionary the word 'renewal' is defined in these words 'among Charismatic Christians, the state or process of being renewed in the Holy Spirit'. Renewal is a process which usually begins with an event. God is always doing new things in our lives and every Christian needs on-going renewal. In 1996 Cardinal Suenens wrote: 'To interpret the Renewal as a movement among other movements is to misunderstand its nature; it is a movement of the Spirit offered to the entire Church and destined to rejuvenate every part of the Church's life.'

Renewal in the Holy Spirit does not happen because we attend a conference or follow a special course or programme. Of course, the Lord uses conferences, courses and programmes, but no-one is renewed except by a sovereign act of God who touches individual lives by the power of his Spirit. In 1976 I did not know why the word 'charismatic' was used, but I quickly discovered that the Holy Spirit freely distributes supernatural gifts or 'charisms' of his choice to those open to receiving them; gifts which are for the blessing and benefit of others and are designed to build up the Church. A reading of Paul's first letter to the Church in Corinth, chapters 12, 13 and 14, provides an eloquent explanation of what these charismatic gifts are and how they are to be used in touching people's lives. At Vatican II, the document on the Church, Lumen Gentium, devotes section 12 to an explanation of the importance of these charisms, as do sections of the Catechism of the Catholic Church and the teachings of several Popes. There are no special, superior people in the Church called 'charismatics', but there are millions of ordinary men and women whose lives have been renewed 'charismatically' – in other words, by a supernatural action of the Holy Spirit with amazing results. This is why the Charismatic Renewal has the support and encouragement of the Catholic hierarchy - fruit and transformed lives speak loudly - and at the time I am writing this, Pope Francis is an eloquent supporter of the work of the Holy Spirit in the Charismatic Renewal. In 1976 I would never have believed how my life would be changed based on what I experienced – after all, I was a 'good' if very nominal Catholic, just like so many others. But personal spiritual transformation is possible for any of us if we are willing to pray with faith 'Come, Holy Spirit!'

Over the years, the Charismatic Renewal in the Catholic Church has taken on a variety of expressions, among them Prayer Groups, Communities, new Ministries and Services, Conferences, Days of Renewal, Seminars, Youth Ministry, Social Action, Spiritual Ecumenism, Discipleship Training, Catechetics and Formation, new Magazines and Books, and much more. The fruit of all this is quite simply millions of changed lives worldwide, conservatively estimated at over 120 million people. Growth continues strongly in Africa, Asia, Eastern Europe and Latin America, whilst in Western Europe and North America the Renewal has largely plateaued and is now seeking to reach more young people.

Our responsibility, as Sue and I, David and Mary have come to know, is to live this grace of the Charismatic Renewal as fully as we can, trusting in the Lord and sharing it with everyone we meet. As St. Paul wrote to Timothy 'Fan into a flame the gift that God gave you when I laid my hands on you' (2 Timothy 1:6), and as Zechariah reminds us: 'Not by might, not by power, but by my Spirit, says the Lord' (Zechariah 4:6). To walk in the Spirit is to walk in the love, the freedom, and the power of God. God willing I hope to do that for the rest of my life, and I pray that you who read this in your own place and country, will continue to do it too, until one day we hear those wonderful words: 'Well done, good and faithful servant' come and join in your master's happiness' (Matthew 25:32).

*Charles Whitehead, President of ICCRS from 1989-1999*

# ELEVEN

# DALLAS, EL PASO, AND JUAREZ

## ....DAVID'S STORY CONTINUED

Tell us Mama how do you know when the food is being multiplied?

The large Mexican lady smiled broadly and replied. 'Well you look at the small amount of food that is left in the bowl, and then you look at the long line of people still waiting to be fed and you just keep spooning the food out, and in the end your arm hurts but there is enough for everyone and a little left for yourself.'

Around 1978 Mary and I were invited along with another couple from Belfast to attend a large Catholic Charismatic Conference in Dallas, Texas. We had never been out of the British Isles before. The other couple were Larry and Mary Kelly. Larry and I were members of the Catholic Charismatic Renewal National Service Committee in Ireland. Larry and Mary were two of our first Catholic friends as we had always been segregated in Northern Ireland.

Larry used expressions which I found strange. Such as when there was something we didn't understand about our faith he would say 'We bow before the Mystery' or when something happened that was painful or irritating he would say 'We offer it up to the Lord'. These things were odd to us and made me smile.

We had been invited to Dallas by a man called Bobby Cavanaugh, who was part of the Renewal in the States and a friend of Larry's. Bobby had come to one of our conferences in Belfast. Later when we got to know him he told us that in his younger days he had been in the U.S. Air force and flown Armed B54 Bombers over Russia in the Cold War of the fifties. Now he was part of the Renewal and helping to organise Charismatic Conferences. He was a large Texan with a slow Texan drawl and greeted us off the plane wearing a ten gallon cowboy hat.

To get to Texas from Belfast we first of all had to fly to Gatwick and then board a large orange jumbo jet for the rest of our journey. Of course being a bit green we got lost in Gatwick and ended up going up and down in the lift a few times trying to find our check-in desk. The company we flew with was called Love Airlines.

I had been asked to give one of the talks at the conference and was quite nervous. There were other well-known speakers there such as Francis McNutt a Dominican priest who had received the Baptism in the Spirit through an Episcopalian lady with gifts in healing. Fr. McNutt was now well-known for his own healing ministry. Many Roman Catholics in the States Religious and Laity had been touched by the move of the Spirit at Duquesne and Notre Dame Universities in the sixties as its effects moved across the States and beyond.

For me the most significant group at the conference was a team from Mexico lead by Fr. Rick Thomas from El Paso. These men were known as the twelve apostles and always carried a satchel in which there was blessed salt for deliverance, holy oil for healing the sick and a copy of the scriptures. None of them could read but miraculously when they opened the word of God they were able to read that.

There was a tremendous work of the Spirit going on in El Paso and across the border in Juarez, Mexico. There were miracles, signs, and wonders taking place on a daily basis as a result of the work of this mission, including food being multiplied as they fed the poor.

These men were the poorest of the poor themselves. At the lunchtime buffet they would stack their plates high with food until Fr. Rick explained that there would be another meal at dinner time and they didn't have to store food for the day. 'Oh they said but you don't have more than one meal in the day.'

There were thousands of people attending the conference and at one session when Fr. Mike Scanlon was preaching things began to go wrong. The P.A. system failed in the middle of his talk and then the lights went out and all the other equipment stopped working. Fr. Rick Thomas said 'this is an attack of the enemy.' The Mexican brothers began to scatter the blessed salt all over the platform and rebuke the devil and all his works. I didn't know what to make of all this but then the lights came back on and the PA system and Fr. Mike was able to continue with his talk.

I was much exercised in my spirit about the Mexican group and felt that the Holy Spirit gave me a word for Fr. Rick about them. The word was that he should not take them on the American 'circuit' but take them home where, as with Mary, these things would be 'hidden in their hearts' for now. Fr. Rick felt that the word was right and that was what he did.

He also invited Mary and me to visit the mission in El Paso and their work across the border in Juarez, Mexico. Bobby Cavanaugh and the Conference bought our air tickets and paid for us to go.

El Paso is just that, it is a passage way between the USA and Mexico on the banks of the Rio Grande. Many of its people are Spanish speaking and Roman Catholic. Mass was celebrated in a large upper room in the mission hall. The only chairs in the room were around the walls for the elderly and expectant mothers. 'These people don't need chairs, David,' Fr. Rick told me, 'They've sat on their butts long enough.'

Fr Rick introduced us and told the people that we had come all the way from Ireland. Everyone cheered. We were quite surprised. Later Rick told us that the people were uneducated and wouldn't even have known where Ireland was. They were so warm and friendly.

The Altar for the mass consisted of two large orange boxes covered in a white linen cloth with a crucifix and candle. The mass in its simplicity and Presence was one of the most beautiful I have ever attended. We were given hospitality by the Mexican lady I mentioned earlier. She told us the story of beginnings of the miracles.

'It was Christmas and we felt that the Lord wanted us to feed the poor, so we cooked dinner. Many people came, more than we had enough for, but we knew that God has told us to do this so we just carried on serving until our arms were sore. We knew then that God had done a miracle. From them on we have seen this happen many times.'

For me the thing that made the whole account authentic to me was that no-one was trying to persuade us of the truth of the miracles that were taking place. You could believe them or not, it made no difference to them.

Next day at five o'clock in the morning we were taken across the Mexican border crossing into Juarez to the early prayer meeting. The area was dry and desert like, near to the city. The team of brothers were already there with their satchels and with many other people dancing and praying fervently in the Spirit. After one or two hours of this the work of the day began.

We were meeting next to the huge municipal dump that served the city of Juarez. Some ladies from El Paso regularly came here to help the people who were actually living on the dump. There were two brothers living in a kind of cave dug into the rubbish mountain. They had made themselves a home from the discarded boxes of television sets and anything else they could find, and foraged for whatever food they could that had been thrown into people's household rubbish. Mama told us their mother had died some years earlier and they had never recovered from the grief. Mama came often to wash and dress their infected feet and pray and try to bring comfort to them. Hundreds of people were living like this on the dump.

There was no clean drinking water available so once a day a lorry would visit selling coca cola to the people. The mission brought food as often as they could and saw the food being multiplied again and again.

In Dallas we had stayed with an executive from one of the big banks. The house was amazing, like a palace in our eyes. The walk-in clothes closets were as big as two or three of our bedrooms at home. For us the culture shock of visiting Dallas had been huge with the large wealthy houses abundance of food big cars and everything else.

In Juarez we swung to the opposite extreme seeing the poorest of the poor and how they lived. It was a real shock to system and yet the Lord, through Fr. Rick and his team, was doing wonderful things among them.

One of Rick's projects was The Lord's Ranch; a huge property in the desert area of New Mexico not many miles across the border. He took us to visit. The vision was to grow food and raise livestock to feed the poor. In the centre was a huge circular paddock where there were animals in the outer circle and a place in the inner circle for worship, prayer and praise. There were also outhouses, accommodation, and other infrastructures.

At the airport in El Paso as we were leaving, Fr. Rick told us the story of once when he was away from the mission there was a special celebration and during the party they ran out of Coca Cola. So they prayed and the Holy Spirit multiplied the Coca Cola. Father Rick had made a personal vow to the Lord that nothing without health or nutritional value would every pass his lips so when he told us what happened he laughingly said,

'It wasn't my Jesus, David.'

What a privilege it was to have seen the miracles God was doing in that place. We went home to Belfast greatly challenged with our heads spinning and our spirits singing,

> 'Lord Renew your wonders in this Our Day as by a New Pentecost.'

From 1964 until his death in 2006 Fr. Rick was the Executive Director of Our Lady's Youth Centre in El Paso Texas. Under his leadership the Centre grew to include different areas of ministry to the poor in Juarez, Mexico including food bank, medical and dental clinics, prison and mental hospital ministries and schools. Dedicated volunteers from both sides of the border continue to run the various ministries.

In 1975 just before we visited, Fr Thomas started The Lord's Ranch east of Vado, New Mexico. Over the years the Ranch has provided recreation and rehabilitation to needy youth, housed hundreds of visitors and run retreats for young and old.

I know that this work continues to this day.

What a privilege we had then to meet such a man and such people of God!

# TWELVE

# ANDY AU'S TESTIMONY

I was born in 1955 in the slums of Calcutta, India. I am mainly Chinese and a quarter Khasi – an Indo-Chinese tribe. My Fathers Father was a rich merchant man from China and had 5 wives and 21 children, he was an ancestor worshipper. My Mothers Mother was from the Khasi Tribe, an Indo-Chinese tribe from the foothills of the Himalayas. The tribe were snake worshippers.

When I was a young baby I became very ill and the doctor was called out. He told my Mum that I wouldn't last the night. Remembering how Hannah dedicated Samuel to the Lord, my Mum prayed out to God saying that if I survived that my life would be dedicated to him. Despite the prognosis I came through.

At the age of 8 my life took a significant turn and we moved out of the slums of India and got a boat to England where we eventually settled in Surrey, one of the wealthiest areas in the UK. This obviously created a lot of culture shock. Everything was different and all my reference points had gone. My father instructed us to forget everything that we'd known and to embrace the English culture, to watch, learn and imitate in order to fit it. I was shy and unconfident and unsure of who I was. Adding these factors along with the Chinese reserve to the English cultural reserve that I'd entered into you can imagine that I was not the natural choice to become a creative free mover.

In fact, I would not have considered myself to be creative in any way. Our family did not have an artistic focus. We did not draw from any of our cultural artistic roots whether they were Chinese, Indian or English. Furthermore, my church background certainly didn't give me much of an understanding of creativity in worship.

In England our family attended a very sound evangelical church. It was all about 'the Word'. Creativity was minimal. The extent of movement vocabulary in worship was basically standing up and sitting down in a meeting. Creativity didn't even figure in my concept of worship. The thought of it wasn't even a possibility in my worldview or my view of God. Let alone moving or dancing in worship.

I came to study as a science and maths teacher at the Teacher Training College in Brighton. Once I was attending a Christian Union meeting and as we were waiting for the meeting to start it was apparent that something special had been planned. We sang a couple of songs of worship. Then everything stopped and when the music began again six or so girls came in wearing wrap around skirts and headscarves and they started to dance. Seeing this within the context of worship basically blew my mind! Internally I questioned:

- 'Is this allowed?'
- 'Is it ok to do this in worship?'
- 'Is this a valid activity within the context of spiritually?'
- 'Is this something that I need to think about or consider?'

I had never seen anything like it. It opened an intellectual window for me, which began my journey into movement in worship.

I had been baptised in the Holy Spirit on the Isle of Wight. The church I belonged to did not believe in the Baptism or using the gifts of the Holy Spirit but I had been exercised about this for some time and could not reconcile the things I found in the scriptures about the Holy Spirit and the views of my church.

Lying in bed one night I saw a sort of vision of the side of a house with a door two storeys up. I heard the Lord say 'Step out of the door and I will hold you up' I stepped out and found myself standing on 'nothing' and speaking in tongues. I also had a strong sense of the verse from Matthew 6.33

> 'seek first the Kingdom of God; and His righteousness and all these things will be given to you as well.'

and Luke 11:13

> 'Which of you fathers if your son asks for a fish will give him a snake instead? Or if he asks for an egg will give

*him a scorpion? If you then though you are evil know how to give good gifts to your children how much more shall your Heavenly Father give the Holy Spirit to those who ask Him!'*

Creativity is making something out of nothing, trusting The God of Creation and what He puts in you. He told me not to trust my senses, eyes ears touch feelings etc but what the Holy Spirit says. To always trust God for everything. He was asking me to trust Him for Anything and Everything.

Several months later another key incident happened. This experience absolutely shocked, intrigued and delighted me. A group of us from the Christian Union went to a tent meeting at a place called In-between Street in Cobham. I walked into the tent where there was a lot of activity going on. We were late and things had already got going, we had missed any explanation that may have been given at the start. The music was pretty loud and right at the front of the tent I saw glimpses of men and women dancing and throwing themselves around. I had never seen anything like this before. I could see that they were worshipping God with absolutely everything. I gripped the chair in front of me really hard. I was totally taken in with what was going on in front of me – transfixed and fascinated.

What really captured me was that these people were totally abandoned to God. They were throwing themselves around and worshipping God - with the songs and yet at the same time with their bodies. That astounded me. I thought Lord God; I want to be able to do that. I want to be able to worship you with absolutely everything.

The experience in Cobham, caught me, it caught me mentally and emotionally and it created a desire in me to worship God with everything. It opened a door in my mind, passion soul and heart. After that I would often hear a prompting during worship times 'Go on then, dance' Every time that happened, I would chicken out saying, 'No, not blooming likely!'

A seed had been planted however and whenever worship reached a really high point I knew that even if I'd sung my head off that this wasn't enough. Singing didn't satisfy my desire to worship God with everything. I even started singing loudly almost shouting in worship, and yet I knew that I wasn't fulfilling this glimpse of worship that I had seen in Cobham.

This continued until a couple of years later in 1979 when finally I gave a different answer! I remember going up to a meeting with a church in Crawley. There must have been approx 150-200 people there. We were worshipping God by singing choruses and in the midst of this worship I heard the audible voice of God say to me, 'Go out to the middle of the room and dance'. I was terrified by the concept, but this time I didn't give my normal response. My desire to worship God with everything met with my fear, creating a dilemma, which caused me to say to God: 'Ok I'll do it, but you've got to give me something'. I had absolutely no idea what to do or how to dance in worship.

The thought and discussion with God that went through my brain was: 'When you give me a prophetic word it starts with a word and grows into sentences and paragraphs. When you give me a prophetic picture, it might start with a twig, but then it grows into a tree. So unless you give me something, to do even if it's small, I'm not going to do anything'. As soon as I said that, I got something, and it was small! As I soon as I asked God he gave me a little picture of me doing a particular movement profile. I thought 'Oh no – I've asked for something small and he's given me something small!' I pictured myself going out into the middle of the room, doing this one move, and then legging it back to my seat, feeling totally stupid and everyone thinking that it was a bit odd, but excusing me with 'don't worry, he's Chinese'.

What actually happened was that I went out into the middle of the room and I did this one movement profile the Holy Spirit had given me but before the end of that move in the same way that I received the first move, I saw in my minds eye, a second move and this second move (thankfully) followed on from the first move. And then at the end of the second move I saw a third move which followed on from the second move. At the end of the third move, I saw a fourth move and it went on like this for about 3-5 minutes, but it felt like hours! Each move coming as I came to the end of the previous move, and each move going seamlessly onto the next one. It was an amazing experience.

At the end of this as I walked back to my seat I felt two things: Firstly, a sense of incredible elation and satisfaction. I had given God my all; I had given him my mind, my emotions and my body. I feel at that point I'd given the Lord everything a bit like 'Romans 12:1 Therefore I urge you brothers in view of God's mercy to offer your bodies as living sacrifices holy and pleasing to God. This is your spiritual act of worship.' And that He had accepted the sacrifice and consumed it. Fire always falls on sacrifice.

There had been total mental engagement. As I was asking God to show me what do next there was a union. On one hand my mind was filled with how amazing God was and on the other hand it was completed engaged with God as he directed the flow of my movements clearly showing me what to do next. There was also an incredible free flow of emotions as I moved. I was totally at peace and lost in God in that place of worship and physically for the first time my body was truly and fully reflecting what was happening in my mind and emotions. There was a sense of total unity, everything aligned and focused on God.

I knew that in this worship I had done what I was created to do; although I had been moving this produced a total stillness, my whole being felt saturated with the stillness that comes from being at one with God. Simultaneously I felt elation, that sense of deep satisfaction that I'd given him everything. I felt totally alive – more alive than ever before!

I had moved in a really unusual way. It was totally different to the girls dancing in the Christian Union and to the men and women throwing their bodies around in Cobham. There was a smooth flow of powerful controlled movement centred on God. It had an oriental feel – which on later reflection perturbed me as I wondered if this was okay. Therefore, later on I went to other Christian leaders including John and Christine Noble to check it out and they reassured me that it was my unique way of worshipping God.

At the end of the meeting many people came up to me. They had been deeply impacted and encouraged by what I had done. I knew something incredible had happened. I didn't know it at the time, but from that one moment of total obedience, my life would never be the same again!

A few weeks later my Mum and my younger brother came down to visit me and my wife in Brighton. Our small fellowship group was meeting so they joined us. There were about twelve of us and we were meeting in the front lounge of a friend's house. Previously I had led my younger brother to the Lord when he was 8 years old, and at this time he must have been 15 years old but he had lost his faith. My Mum had been in China for six months and my younger brother had gone out to join her for the last six weeks of her time there. In the middle of the meeting, which we didn't have music at, I heard God say to me, 'Get up and move'. I thought 'Oh no – my Mum's here, my younger brother's here, Lord have mercy!'

He didn't, and I still felt prompted to dance, so I went out and worshipped God with movement. Then I sat down and the meeting carried on. At the end of the meeting my brother came to me and said: 'You know those people who were speaking as if they were God (the prophetic) they're crazy. And you know those people that were speaking gobbledygook (people speaking in tongues) well that's just gobbledygook.' Then he said, 'and do you know what you were doing?' All that I was able to say was that I was worshipping God. And he said, 'But do you know what you were doing?' and I said 'well I was dancing' and he said 'you don't really know what you were doing, do you?' I had no idea what he was thinking about what I had just done, but in the light of his opinion of the other activities in the meeting I was guessing that he was going to ridicule me. At this point I was getting really annoyed with my brother; it is very disrespectful to speak to an elder sibling in this way in a Chinese family, so in a frustrated way I said, 'Okay, you tell me, what do you think I was doing?'

So he said, 'Every morning over the last six weeks Mum and I have been going out into the park in China and we've been doing a series of moves and you've just done that whole sequence of moves that we have been doing in China.' He went through and named some of the moves that I had done. The moves that he had been learning in China were Tai Chi Chuan and he said to me 'I know you know tiddlysquat about Tai Chi Chuan!!'

After that my brother came back to God and has now for many years been a missionary in Cambodia, which is amazing. I believe that this experience provoked him to think and was part of a whole chain of events that brought him back to God, eventually pushing him out into the mission field. Now if this was the only fruit that had happened through me moving to worship God it would all have been worth it. However, this was just the beginning. We've seen people healed, set free, brought into the presence of God in a deeper way, all of this through movement in the context of worshipping God.

We sometimes have 'drumming and movement' worship times in the Streets in Brighton. Once a man came and stood in front of me watching. He said:

> 'I am here because I 'felt' you move when I was in the next street so I came through to see who it was. He was familiar with a martial arts discipline called Whynchun and he said. 'When the Masters move you can feel them a whole mile away.' What are you doing? 'I am moving and worshipping God.' I said.

It is said that the occult only imitates the reality of the things of the Spirit, like fortune telling etc only imitates the foretelling prophetic ministry. Who knows what a depth and width there are to the wonders of God waiting to be expressed through His people. The whole creation is groaning; Romans 8:18, 19:

*'I consider that our present sufferings are not worth comparing with the glory that will be revealed in us. The creation waits in eager expectation for the sons of God to be revealed.'*

And who knows what glory the Holy Spirit is waiting to reveal through His sons and daughters. The Holy Spirit has conceived the Creative Word of God Jesus Christ THE WORD in each one of His children just as He conceived Him in the womb of Mary. Perhaps the time is coming soon when He will be fully born through His bride the church so that the world may see His Glory.

The Holy Spirit conceives the incarnation of the creative Word of God Jesus Christ within us and we bring to birth the thoughts and heart of God. When I give myself over to the Holy Spirit in worship through movement Christ has been 'written' into my body and I am prophetically speaking 'The Word' through movement.

*Andy Au, 2017*
*Andy Au is the Founding Director of 'Movement in Worship', a ministry begun the 1980's. Since then he has played a pioneering role in dance and creativity in worship in the United Kingdom and beyond. He is currently based in Brighton.*

# THIRTEEN

# A Very English Way into the Renewal of the Holy Spirit

## Fr. Peter Hocken

I was ordained a Catholic priest for the diocese of Northampton in February, 1964. I had been excited by the ministry of St John XXIII and the work of the Second Vatican Council. I was intellectually gifted and oriented, so I imagined my ministry as a priest would be bringing the teaching of the Council to the Catholic people – the teaching on the Church, on primacy and collegiality, on the role of the laity, on the Scriptures, and on ecumenism. My first full assignment was to a parish in Corby, Northamptonshire, an industrial town where many of the men worked shifts in the steel works and there was hardly any middle class. It was not a propitious environment to explain the theology of Vatican Two. This was a first dent in my assumption that progress for the Church meant theological progress.

After four years I was invited to teach moral theology at Oscott College, the seminary of the Birmingham Archdiocese. As I had no greater education in this subject than any other priest completing the basic seminary course, I asked the Archbishop for the chance to do further studies. This was too difficult to arrange immediately, so I taught at

Oscott for one year, and then went to Rome for a two-year course in moral theology. During my second year in Rome (1970 – 71) I was living at the English College, which was a stimulating environment spiritually and theologically. I prayed with a few other students occasionally on a spontaneous basis. It was not charismatic, but there was a definite sense that Someone Else was active in the prayer besides us. The other factor that prepared me for the Renewal was reading the book Catholic Pentecostals by Kevin and Dorothy Ranaghan. The shared prayer together had made me open for what the Ranaghans were describing and I began to thirst for it.

One day off I went out to the mountains with a fellow student and we prayed for the Holy Spirit. Nothing seemed to happen. I must have asked the Lord about this disappointment, for I received the definite impression we had not been asking correctly. We had been praying a kind of 'Zap us' prayer as though the Lord had not given us anything significant so far. I was reminded of this verse: 'Have no anxiety about anything, but in everything by prayer and thanksgiving let your requests be made known to God.' (Phil. 4: 6).

My opportunity came soon after my return to England. I made my first ever trip across the Atlantic in the summer of 1971, but had no contact with Renewal. But as soon as I returned to Oscott in September 1971, I saw an advertisement for a week-end on prophecy at Spode House in

Staffordshire to be led by Fr Simon Tugwell, op. Simon was at that time publishing a series of articles in New Blackfriars that would be published in book form the following year under the title *Did You Receive the Spirit?* Several important things happened at this week-end. It was the first time I had encountered the spiritual gifts of 1 Cor. 12:8–10. The participants were not all Catholics. Simon invited all participants one evening to use the Hawkesyard Priory church at Spode as 'a praying space' being free to pray and relate to the Lord as we were led. Fr Simon's talks were profound, combining references to the Desert Fathers and early Dominicans with some to 20th-century Pentecostals. I heard how several of those present had received the Spirit through fellowship with English Pentecostals either at a weekly prayer meeting in Denton, near Oxford, or at Hockley Pentecostal Church in Birmingham. There was no reference to the USA and to Duquesne 1967.

At the Spode week-end, I met several people from a prayer group that met each Thursday evening in Edgbaston, Birmingham in the home of Gae Twomey, who had received the Spirit at Hockley. From this point I attended the Edgbaston group regularly – it was mostly Catholic, but with a few Anglicans – and I felt quite at home. The next Saturday I was there again together with Gae and two Dominican brothers from Oxford who were familiar with the Denton prayer meeting. These three had already entered into this Pentecostal experience. As we prayed, the others began singing in the Spirit, and I immediately knew that I could join in. So I began singing in tongues without any imposition of hands, or prayer for the Holy Spirit. This act of faith opened a new chapter in my life, of which more in a moment. The following Saturday these friends took me to Hockley Pentecostal Church, in a run-down inner city suburb of Birmingham. That evening was an eye-opener for me, a Catholic priest teaching moral theology in the diocesan seminary, another dent in my theology-dominated life.

We had to enter the church through a tunnel (I think some reconstruction had been happening). Entering the tunnel, the noise of music and joy-filled praise grew louder. I thought it must have been like this for the early Christians entering the Roman catacombs. The service was led by two remarkable women, known as Miss Reeve and Miss Fisher, both in their 70s, who had pastored this congregation for over thirty years. Saturday evenings was Revival Time to welcome all comers. Visitors from other churches were encouraged to go to their own church on Sunday. The congregation was an extraordinary mixture of races and colours, of those who dressed well and those who did not smell too good, of university lecturers and patients from the local psychiatric hospital. The music was lively with trumpet and trombone. It was unlike any other service (Anglican or free church) that I had experienced.

Miss Reeve and Miss Fisher complemented each other perfectly. Miss Reeve did not shout like Miss Fisher. She was far less demonstrative, a dignified and alert presence on the platform, giving rich prophecies full of biblical allusions in the language of the authorised version of King James. Miss Fisher was more energetic, dancing with power (I don't think I've seen this anywhere else since); her laying hands on people was no delicate gesture. Though I never had lengthy conversations with them, they were my first mentors in the ways of the Spirit. They had a remarkable openness to the Holy Spirit, but they conveyed the sense of knowing exactly what they were about. This was important for me encountering spiritual phenomena, good and bad, for the first time. The two ladies were remarkably open to Catholics and once when a visiting preacher made some anti-Catholic remarks, they invited a sister to come up and share the wonderful things the Lord was doing among the Roman Catholics.

My experiences in Edgbaston and Hockley changed my whole approach to ministry. This change happened immediately in relation to my preaching. Instead of preparing sermons at my desk, and trying to make my messages interesting, I began to prepare in the chapel, asking the Lord what He wanted me to say to these people on this occasion. This quickly produced a new fruitfulness. I had a new level of love and zeal for the Lord, and of thirst for the Word of God. I had discovered the Lord who speaks to his people.

All this was right at the beginnings of the Renewal in Britain. At this point the Renewal was often called the Catholic Pentecostal movement, a phrase that captured what we were experiencing. Although I went to one of two of the early Days of Renewal in London, the major input for the Edgbaston prayer group was coming from Simon Tugwell week-ends at Spode House, and from Hockley. Maybe the British origins were unique in this: having one indigenous strand arising from contact with local Pentecostals, and the other arriving from the United States. Simon Tugwell was never at ease with the latter, and as the Renewal became more organised he pulled back. At that point I knew I could not pull back, but I struggled for some time as to the right way forward. We, priests included, were really all novices in the things of the Spirit.

In our small circle, we emphasised the freedom of the Spirit, looking down upon more organised forms of Renewal. We had no regular format for the weekly prayer meeting, we just began praying and seeking to be led by the Spirit. So the pattern of the meeting could vary greatly from week to week. We didn't have formal teaching, though there could be shared reflections with some substance. We avoided Life in the Spirit seminars, not approving of 'packaged' Renewal. It was only later that I realised our pattern was only possible because we were a group of less than twenty people meeting in the room of a private house set aside as a prayer room.

One of the factors that helped me get beyond this negativity to structured renewal was the realisation after a time that we were no longer introducing people to the Pentecost experience. From about 1974, there were regular Days of

Renewal in Birmingham, in which I participated and prayed for people to receive the Spirit. I have avoided using the term 'baptism in the Spirit' as we never spoke then in those terms. We had contact with some charismatic Anglicans, and there was a charismatic Anglican parish nearby in Harborne. These contacts also helped to broaden my view. It was in 1975 at a national Renewal conference held at Hopwood Hall, Manchester, with Fr Francis MacNutt as main speaker that I heard the Lord telling me to identify with the Catholic charismatic renewal whatever its limitations. The Lord was freeing me from a rather superior and judgmental attitude that had prevented me from entering fully into the charismatic movement as it was spreading across the churches.

The Lord had put unity on my heart back in 1955, before even the Council had been called. I was excited by the opening of the Catholic Church to ecumenism at the Council. After my ordination in 1964, I quickly became involved in ecumenical relations. For these reasons knowing this grace of Pentecost was being poured out across the Christian world, I immediately sensed the importance for Christian unity of the charismatic renewal. But with my experience of Pentecost, there was a whole new Holy Spirit dimension to my ecumenical understanding.

Because of my experience at Hockley Pentecostal Church I knew that the charismatic movement would not have been possible without the Pentecostal movement: I knew that we should honour the Pentecostals for their witness to the power of the Holy Spirit. I sensed that the instinct of many charismatic Christians, not only Catholics, to distance themselves from the Pentecostals was not from the Lord. For many, it seemed as though the main lesson to learn from the Pentecostals was to avoid their excesses. There was a parallel trend on the Pentecostal side, of caution about the charismatics, as though we were getting Pentecost on the cheap – without radical change. As I entered more deeply into the charismatic renewal, I knew that I had to contend for the ecumenical character of this outpouring of the Holy Spirit. So it is a great joy in my latter years to see how Pope Francis enters freely and with joy into fellowship with Pentecostal pastors and to hear him emphasising the inherently ecumenical character of this work of the Holy Spirit.

*Fr Peter is a British theologian and historian of the Catholic Charismatic Renewal and the Pentecostal Movement in the twentieth century.*

## FOURTEEN

# THE BEGINNING OF A NEW DAWN

## MYLES DEMPSEY

Charismatic Renewal first came to England in 1971 through an American salesman, Bob Balcombe, and began to take root gradually over the following three years. A large prayer group was established at Westminster Cathedral and a fledgling Day of Renewal developed, mainly through the encouragement given by Dom Benedict Heron, Fr Michael Gwinnell, and Richard Connor, an ecumenical Anglican and ex Lieutenant Colonel.

The 1970s and early 80s represent the halcyon days of the Renewal. It was a period of innocent excitement, lively expectation and great trust, joy, love and genuine friendship. New things were happening. There was a sense of great hope for the Church and many of us were eager to play our part in bringing about some very necessary changes. We had an acute awareness of the Holy Spirit's presence and action, and a deeper understanding and appreciation of what the Church was meant to be, coupled with a true experience of genuine ecumenical encounter.

Days of Renewal were springing up in various areas, and

developed mainly through the encouragement given by Ian Petit OSB. For a while I acted as Chairman of the Westminster Day of Renewal, and during that period we began to see the need for meaningful ecumenical engagement. One important development arising out of all this was the formation of an organisation which we named 'All Saints Together'. Leaders in The House Church movement featured greatly in this endeavour, including David Matthews and his wife Mary, who had a clear understanding of what ecumenism meant. The House Church people provided a large choir, while the Catholic Day of Renewal took care of the finances and organisation. In all, this was a very successful venture, and even a member of the English hierarchy played an active role.

I became involved with the Charismatic Renewal on 3rd January 1973 through a meeting with Lalage Hall, a friend from the days when we were both involved in the Catholic Evidence Guild. She took me to a small prayer group in Soho. I had already read part of a book written by Kevin and Dorothy Ranahan, and was so eager to be baptised in the Holy Spirit that I had considered travelling to America in order to have the experience. The little Soho group prayed over me during my first visit and my life was transformed from that moment. I felt as though my entire internal self was being opened up and something indescribable was happening to me. It seemed as though a 'major surgery' operation was being performed. I experienced a big change taking place, leaving me somewhat disorientated – so much so that on a short journey from Soho to Kensington at midnight (both points north of the River Thames) I drove across four bridges, travelling over Westminster Bridge on the wrong side of the road. I was experiencing a form of mild inebriation of the Spirit. A pronounced sense of elation continued for some weeks. Many significant events took place within me, all leading to a deepening of the God Encounter associated with Baptism of the Holy Spirit.

Shortly after that, I routinely went to Confession in my own parish church. No sooner had I knelt in front of the Blessed Sacrament to perform the act of penance than the tabernacle seemed to come alive and began to exert a strong attraction towards me. My soul was 'leaping out of my body' and I felt impelled to move forward so as to put my arms around the tabernacle, but was restrained only by the awareness of other people's presence in the Church. I next heard some keys being rattled by the person locking up, and quickly left for home to continue praying at the same deep level. I went upstairs to be alone in our bedroom and knelt at the bedside with a crucifix standing in front of me on the bed. Suddenly the whole aspect of that crucifix changed. It was no longer a piece of wood with a plastic figure nailed to it, but it was a life-sized cross with the living, writhing Christ nailed to it. It was as though he eagerly wanted to embrace me, but was restrained by the nails. He showed great intensity in his desire. How long this whole experience lasted could not be measured, as it was outside the world of time.

Before I joined the Soho prayer group, some members had

established the practice of travelling to Oxfordshire on Friday nights to participate in a Pentecostal prayer meeting which took place in the summerhouse of Joan Steele who ran an ecumenical prayer group there together with her prayer partner, Fred Smith, who had a recognised healing ministry. Joan's activities had already drawn the attention of some Catholic theologians, notably Simon Tugwell OP, who wrote a very popular book 'Did you receive the Spirit?' arising out of his experience with her group.

Attending the Oxfordshire group made a deep impact on my life. Joan was a Jewish lady who had become a Pentecostal Christian some years earlier. She was a very good teacher. There are two things in particular that I learnt through contact with that group. I found that the stereotype description of Pentecostalism fell far short of the reality, and it was there that I experienced true ecumenism, as the group was composed of people from a great variety of denominations. After I had been attending the Soho group gatherings for a short while, I was asked to become the leader, and it was then that I greatly benefited from the Oxford experience, where there was much emphasis on the importance of loud praise, use of charismatic gifts and the freedom the Spirit brings.

Having a prayer group in the heart of Soho represented a considerable challenge because of the reputation of the area and the immoral practices carries out there. Before I joined, the group had already established the practice of regularly praying for the spiritual cleansing of the district, but seemed to be ineffective until one night when I received a word from the Lord telling me, 'Pray this: "Lord, dismantle the edifice of corruption in Soho." I prayed accordingly, not knowing that at that precise moment a late-night jury returned a verdict of 'Guilty' for a man who had been arraigned before the court on charges arising out of contravention of certain laws connected with the Obscene Publication Act. A prison sentence of eight years was imposed.

The following morning the front page of the Daily Mirror carried a banner headline: 'Vice Empire Crumbles', paraphrasing the very words I had used in my prayer the previous night. All strip club and porn shop managers pulled the shutters down on their premises and disappeared. The wife of the jailed man became very angry because her husband, who was the corruption king, had been paying out large sums of money to members of the police force of all ranks up to the level of Commander to ensure protection against prosecution, and now felt greatly let down.

She decided to 'spill the beans' and expose the police, resulting in the Commander and accomplices being also jailed. A fresh police force was installed to continue investigations, but this police force gave so much time to examining the past misdemeanours that the necessary street patrolling required for ongoing activities was neglected and gradually the immoral establishments cautiously reopened.

It was at this point that we decided to carry out our own 'Spiritual Patrolling' in the streets. Our procedure entailed sending selected members of the group on a prayer walk through the affected areas two by two (one man and one woman) looking quite innocent, while praying, planting Miraculous Medals and spreading blessed salt. On the very first occasion, while all our 'vigilantes' were gathered together, I noticed that a certain premises, which had previously closed down after our prayer had now reopened with aggressive displays. My immediate reaction was to raise my hand and, with the best of intentions, said: 'Lord, let the fire of your Spirit fall on this place.' That night a fire broke out and the building was totally destroyed, but with no casualties. The site was eventually bought by a developer who erected a block of offices. How great God is! We must at all times simply 'Do whatever he tells us' without hesitation.

In 1975, while praying in my parish church, I received a clear word telling me to go to the forthcoming international Charismatic Conference in Rome taking my wife and three children with me. I was penniless at the time. We prayed in faith and the money came just in time.

During the Conference we had the most wonderful experiences of our lives and were the only complete family present at the Conference of ten thousand participants representing sixty-four countries.

In 1976, while again penniless, I was asked to go to Paris to meet a young Jewish man, Jean Rodolphe Kars, who was one of the foremost classical pianists in the world. His life was in turmoil and he had no faith whatsoever. After a lengthy discussion he agreed that I could pray over him (he was desperate). As I prayed for him, I received a word of knowledge telling me that he would be baptised and that he would become a priest. He was subsequently baptised in the Sacre Coeur and commenced studies for the priesthood. He eventually became chaplain at Paray le Monial, where he has been serving for over thirty years. I believe he is a sign from God foreshadowing the day when the Jewish race will accept Jesus Christ as the true Messiah.

On the feast of Blessed Dominic Barberi, August 26th 1985, at the end of a large charismatic conference in Ars I went on a walk in the countryside and discovered a wayside shrine on a narrow road leading to the village.

It was while I was kneeling there, thanking God for the experience of the conference, that I said to the Lord 'It is wonderful to see what you have been doing in Ars during the past days, but this is France. What about England? Should something like this be taking place in England? Would you want such an event to take place in England?' I was taken by surprise by the suddenness of the Lord's reply; 'Walsingham – New Dawn'.

I understood this to mean 'Learn from what you have seen and when you go home establish a conference along the same lines with the title 'New Dawn'. It must take place in Walsingham.

On returning to England I first approached the Shrine Director (Fr Peter Allan) who cautiously gave consent to the project and then I began to tackle the organisational and logistical problems, with no funds except £20 in coins in a jam jar on my office table.

Of course, I realised that I would have to inform the Bishop of East Anglia to seek his approval. I delayed before doing this as I knew the Bishop to be a very practical man who would want assurances on a variety of issues and I was being careful to have everything in place before he could ask for details of our arrangements.

In the meantime I had arranged for a quantity of publicity material to be printed and delivered to a prayer group leader in Norfolk who would take care of the posters for us until the time arrived for them to be posted in appropriate places. Due to some miscommunication the prayer group leader understood that the posters were for immediate display and commenced pasting them to lamp posts etc.

Then one day Bishop Clarke, while motoring in the countryside, saw a poster nailed to a tree announcing the forthcoming New Dawn Conference.

A priest who accompanied him at the time warned me as to

the bishop's immediate reaction. He said that apoplexy would be a mild term to use in describing the outburst that followed. Almost beside himself with rage, the Bishop declared 'Why don't I know about this? Who are these people? Conference in Walsingham! Out of the question, and totally against the tradition; Pilgrimage maybe, but Conference – never! Five days duration - ridiculous! One day probably, or two at most.'

The priest who told me this gave me to understand that I could expect rough treatment when I would eventually meet the Bishop.

Some time during the 2nd week of September I received a phone call from the National Service Committee telling me that they had a problem. They had been approached by Cardinal Suenens who explained to them that he would be visiting England to participate in the annual Conference of the Ecumenical Society of the Blessed Virgin Mary of which he was co-founder, with the late Martin Gillet.

As the Conference was due to finish on Friday September 19th he had arranged to meet with Cardinal Hume on Saturday 20th, but had just been told that the time for this meeting would have to be cancelled as Cardinal Hume was being called away from London for this particular date.

This, Cardinal Suenens told the N.S.C., would leave him a totally free day on 26th September. If he could be of any help to the Renewal in London, he was ready to serve in whatever capacity the occasion might present. As the N.S.C. members would be gathered together for their own conference in the north of England during that weekend there was little they could do.

When asked if I could provide some worthwhile event and play host to the Cardinal, I replied that I could not help in that way as I would be in Norwich at this time. After that I had a sudden thought – perhaps I could arrange for the Cardinal to take my place as speaker at Norwich and so solve all the problems. I then got in touch with the organisers of the Norwich event, who were delighted at the possibility of inviting the Cardinal.

I next telephoned Cardinal Suenens' priest secretary in Italy who in turn consulted the Cardinal, who was happy to oblige.

When I received a return telephone call from the priest secretary I felt I could now relax, but soon became anxious when I reflected on what I had done. I said to myself 'This great man is a Prince of the Church, one of the principal auditors for the Vatican Council, Archbishop of the very important diocese of Malines, one of the most widely known men in the world, and here I am taking him along to an out-of-the-way city in England to address a small number of local people. What have I done? But it is too late of other arrangements now. I'm sure I will be considered crazy.'

Early in the morning of 20th September I was considering how to make the day as fulfilling as possible for the Cardinal and a thought came into my head. (I now know it was an inspiration of the Holy Spirit.) Perhaps to pass the day I could persuade the Cardinal to visit the Shrine of Our Lady of Walsingham on the way to Norwich. Whereupon I telephoned the Shrine Director, who said this would be a wonderful idea, and that he would arrange lunch for us at the Marist house and take the Cardinal to the Anglican Shrine also, which would be most appropriate as Cardinal Suenens was well known among Anglicans because of his efforts to establish ecumenical dialogue.

When I arrived at Archbishop's House in Westminster to collect the Cardinal I asked him if he would like to visit the Shrine at Walsingham and he was quite amenable. (I avoided telling him of the long detour involved.)

As we were approaching Walsingham I debated with myself as to whether I should first enter the village and introduce the Shrine Director, but decided to go straight to the Slipper Chapel.

After parking the car on arrival, I began to feel anxious again. What would the Cardinal think of this little place? Knowing that there were two major national shrines in Belgium which he would have visited often, as well as leading pilgrimages to Lourdes and other places, with gatherings of several thousands, what would he say now? I escorted him to the

Slipper Chapel and, as he entered, I boldly said, 'This, Your Eminence, is the National Shrine of Our Lady for England.' I wondered what his reaction would be when he saw a building with a capacity for 20 seats, but he immediately spotted something which I had not noticed. There was a tiny plaque on the wall, bearing an inscription which told him that the ashes of Martin Gillet, his co-founder, were contained there. The Cardinal prayed for a moment for the soul of his friend and blessed the ashes. He then turned to me and said in a very profound way, 'If for no other reason, it has been well worth my while to come here today, and I stress 'for no other reason'. I breathed a sigh of relief and silently said 'Thank you, Lord.'

It had been arranged that when the Cardinal had finished his talk in Norwich he would celebrate Mass with the people he had addressed, using the main altar in the Cathedral, before retiring to the adjacent Clergy House where he and I, together with his secretary, would have our evening meal and spend the night there before travelling back to London on the following morning.

Shortly after the Mass had begun, Bishop Clarke came into the Cathedral and sat on the Bishop's throne. The Cardinal was a very good liturgist and celebrated Mass beautifully (as the Bishop later acknowledged.)

I knew that when Mass ended I would have to face the Bishop and give an account of my activities, but the Holy Spirit and Our Lady had better ideas.

As the Cardinal processed back to the sacristy the Bishop followed him and they had a conversation together, after which the arrangements for our evening meal in Clergy House were cancelled and we were invited by Bishop Clarke to accompany him to his residence some miles away and enjoy a meal with him in Porrington.

We travelled in one car, the Bishop driving with the Cardinal in the front passenger seat and the two secretaries with me in the back seat. As we journeyed along the Cardinal and Bishop were engaged in a very lively conversation together while the rest of us listened to some amusing exchanges as the two senior clerics reminisced about their time together at the Vatican Council.

When we arrived we were treated to a sumptuous meal, with good conversation as a bonus. When the meal ended the Bishop motioned for us to sit before a very inviting log fire while the dishes were cleared away.

The Cardinal was now in very good form and the Bishop was quite animated. We all had a whirlwind, wide-ranging conversation touching on many aspects of life in the Church. The Cardinal was a brilliant raconteur and told many amusing stories which left the Bishop in very good humour.

After a while the Cardinal said 'We've had an excellent round-up of the news so far, is there anything we've left out. What about Medjugorje?' to which the Bishop replied quickly, by saying 'I've never been there.' 'Neither have I.' said the Bishop's secretary and 'Neither have I,' said the Cardinal's secretary.

Then the Bishop's secretary looked at me and said 'I believe you've been there.' When I acknowledged that I had gone there on more than one occasion, the Cardinal said 'Well, tell us about it.' When I had given a thorough account of my experiences and spoke enthusiastically of my belief in the authenticity of the apparitions, the Cardinal said, with a benevolent smile on his face, 'You are a very good propagandist,' adding 'but leave yourself just that much room, in case the Vatican says no.' as he held up the thumb and forefinger of his right hand with a tiny gap of about one eighth of an inch between them.

Then suddenly turning fully towards me he said, apropos of nothing, 'Now what about this Charismatic Conference you are planning for Walsingham, how are things going?' I immediately replied 'Oh, everything is going fine, Your Eminence, our plans are well advanced and we are hoping that you might come and speak for us yourself.'

'Well, if God spares me I would be happy to do so,' said the Cardinal. 'What an excellent idea!' said the Bishop, looking quite excited at the prospect. Under my breath I was saying 'Thank you Lord. Thank you Mary.'

The Bishop never raised the matter again and we were able

# THE BEGINNING OF A NEW DAWN

to mount the first New Dawn Conference without any further worries.

In the event the Cardinal was not able to attend, but he had done all that was required to clear the way for us.

The Bishop drove us back to the Clergy House in Norwich, where we spent the night before taking off for a scheduled meeting with Cardinal Hume. I imagine that Cardinal Suenens would not have missed the opportunity of informing the Cardinal Archbishop of Westminster about the forthcoming Pilgrimage/Conference at Walsingham.

The Lord plans everything well in advance. We must always trust him, and never cease to praise him!

*Myles Dempsey, Founder of the New Dawn Conferences*

## FIFTEEN

# CELEBRATE LEGACY
# SUE WHITEHEAD

The Southampton Charismatic Conference had been started by local prayer groups and in 1980, my husband, Charles, was invited to take on the Chairmanship. I helped with the bookings! It was a very successful conference catering for up to 400 people aged 16 and above but by the end of the 1980s we began to sense that we should really be offering something for the whole family, including the children. We were encouraged in this by a prophetic word brought to us by one of our speakers, David Matthews, and so took the decision to call others to a weekend of discernment about the way ahead. As a result, the search began for a new family-friendly venue for a week-long residential conference.

At first we thought we might be able to link up with Spring Harvest Conferences but this proved too complicated so Charles wrote to every holiday camp in England to ask if there was a possibility of taking over a site for Easter Week. We only had about £400 in the kitty, but felt sure that we were in God's will and everything would work out. Letters arrived in reply to our question, but the only positive one was from the manager of the John Fowler Holiday Park in

Ilfracombe. He began his letter with these words: 'The Lord has been prompting me for some time to offer our Holiday Park for a Christian Conference.' A few days later we were in Ilfracombe to visit the John Fowler site. The manager, Clive Nottage, a Reader in the local Anglican Church, had already checked out Ilfracombe College 400 yards down the road, to see if we could hire it for our meetings and he had, of course, worked out what renting his whole Holiday Park would cost us. It was an excellent venue for us, self-catering holiday chalets, a shop, takeaways, a restaurant, a bar area with a dance floor and very friendly staff. And the price for the site? Well, we could always sell our house if we didn't attract enough people to cover the costs!

So CELEBRATE 94 was launched and almost 900 people arrived on Easter Sunday afternoon in pouring rain and sleet. It was very cold and most of the chalets lost their electricity the first evening, but we survived. The Conference was a great success and financially we were in the black having based our budget on 750 delegates. There were streams for the children, special programmes for the young people and adults, worship groups, mime artists, guest speakers, a bookshop, the evening 'fringe' and the local bishop celebrating our opening Eucharist.

That's how it all began and now, this year (2017) we are privileged to also have 13 non-residential CELEBRATE weekends all over the UK, all following the CELEBRATE vision and designed to bring folk to a closer, more personal walk with God. They are amazing; run by local teams and having 300-550 people attending.

Many of the children who have reached Joel's Bar, the 16+ stream at CELEBRATE, describe themselves as 'Celebrate Babies' and some of these young people consider it a privilege to help at the regional weekends. The Celebrate leadership team recognised there was a challenge to equip these new young leaders and formation was needed to help them take the step from receiving to giving. We needed a structured approach so that they were properly supported not just 'thrown in the deep end' and so we launched RELEASE – to release them into the gifts which God has given them. The programme has four contact events during the year; one week at Worth Abbey and two subsequent weekends as well as a service project which means they really get involved in a variety of activities. Through the marvel of the internet a 'cyber' community is created during the year and support and friendships shared, as well as the swapping of thoughts and advice. The young leaders are given a wide variety of spiritual and practical teaching at each of the events and supplied with a number of resources; books, magazine subscriptions, accountability, partner guidance, daily scripture readings and a website with downloadable podcasts. This year will see us starting our fourth course for about 30 young Celebrators aged 18-24 years old. We are so proud of them as they mature into amazing people – gifted speakers, worship leaders and organisers, generally discerning the call that God has on their lives.

A very important part of the CELEBRATE vision is to include among those invited as Speakers, men and woman from the Protestant, Pentecostal, and Non-Denominational charismatic churches and fellowships, so that we benefit from their gifts and therefore promote unity among Christians.

Being an Anglican myself I have felt privileged to help organise this wonderful 'getting together' but it is not without painful moments. We celebrate Mass every day and at the moment of distribution I cannot receive but have to go instead for a blessing, and I am not alone in that as many marriages these days are 'mixed'!. This is part of our life - a pain experienced at each Mass – which Charles and I accept as part of our walk with God.

So let me share with you something which happens at every Ilfracombe CELEBRATE. At the end of the week we always have a Non-Catholic communion service, usually celebrated by one of our main ecumenical speakers. We invite all the delegates to join us as a witness to our unity across the denomination divide and to support those delegates who have attended Mass each day without receiving the Lord, and many people do come. If it is an Anglican service it is almost word perfect for Mass and this surprises many – so many of us don't step outside our traditions into others and we often do not know how other Christians celebrate their faith. At the time of distribution we ask everyone to come forward up the centre aisle and either receive the host and chalice or to turn to the side where they will receive a blessing – either from the celebrant or myself. It really is momentous for many people as they often feel that they have attended Mass (word wise) and, often for the first time, they have to turn away from the Lord's presence and be blessed instead. At that moment they often experience the pain of the divided body for the first time and their hearts are open in a new way to the desire for reconciliation amongst God's children. We have been aware at those moments of the Holy Spirit sweeping over us so that in our grief we long to grow closer and, we often ask forgiveness for the divisions that we, personally, have caused or furthered.

Because Charles and I are from different traditions we are very aware of the divisions in God's family. We feel that God has called us to work for reconciliation between Christians and that usually means witnessing to the presence of the Holy Spirit in our lives and recognising His presence in others. We have been blessed so often by others giving freely of themselves to help us on our walk, that we long for all His children to know their brothers and sisters better, to accept each other and to build relationships with them.

As I said earlier, very few of us step outside our traditions and why should we? It's often enough to 'get on' with those around us and not look for additional relationship problems! But to witness to the world about our wonderful God, we need to show His love and that should really bind us closer together.

*'A new commandment I give you: Love one another. As I have loved you, so you must love one another. By this will all men know that you are my disciples, if you love one another.'* John 13:34

This is our desire – to show that we do not have to agree with everything to live in harmony. In fact, Charles and I manage that quite well! We love being together, learning to understand each other's foibles, compromising on the non-essential elements of life and accepting each other totally because we love each other so much. We long to live like that with all our Christian brothers and sisters – you are all important because you are and the desire is the precursor of the act.

We started CELEBRATE as a conference where families could experience a church community – a week of living together, worshipping, studying, and generally having a good time. For many children to discover that it was all right to be a Christian – actually quite cool! All of us have the opportunity to grow in our faith and we have had the joy of seeing many Celebrators being received into the church after they have spent time with us and experienced the love, joy and encouragement of the other delegates.

*Sue is the co-founder of the Celebrate conferences with her husband, Charles.*

## SIXTEEN

# MARY MATTHEWS
# SPRINGS OF JOY

When my husband David was baptised in the Holy Spirit he received the gift of tongues. When he went home he spent the rest of the night reading the Bible and praying in his new language. He read that there were many Gifts of the Spirit and so, being my David, he asked God for all of them. David is a person who commits one hundred and fifty per cent to everything he does.

We were a 'couple' at the time so also, being David; he wanted to pray for me immediately to have the same experience. I was not so sure about the whole thing. As a child I had a family history of some occult practices. My great aunt read tea-leaves and often read mine. I also remember once being involved in an Ouija board session and there were some other fortune telling type things that were practiced around Halloween. Superstition is a big thing in Ireland and these things had left me fearful of anything 'supernatural' especially some Being who had the word Ghost in His name.

David has also (unwisely) told me that the Holy Ghost could come 'upon me' during the night. Well, that just about finished it. He was all right in hymns in church but I certainly did not want this Holy Spirit 'turning' up in the middle of the night.

After a few years however, through prayer, ministry the Lord set me free from the negative effects of the occult and by the time we took up our pastorate I also was baptised in the Holy Spirit. Tongues came gradually, mostly by faith. I didn't experience the great gushing stream that others have, I simply speak and I know that it is the Holy Spirit speaking through me.

I find my own gifting seems to be mainly in wisdom and prophecy, also in teaching and writing. I also receive many 'rhema' words from the Lord; Living words that leap out at me from the scriptures or words that the Holy Spirit brings from my memory, and anoints. Words that come straight from God's heart to my heart to meet a need or particular circumstance in my life. For example when the Lord spoke to us about moving back into Belfast with our two babies, Avril and Joanne, at the height of the troubles these were the words He gave me: (Isaiah 54:14)

> *In righteousness you will be established:*
> *tyranny will be far from you.*
> *You will have nothing to fear*
> *Terror will be far removed;*
> *It will not come near you.*

In the times of terrorist attacks in Northern Ireland it was good to know that God was protecting us and to have that foundation from the Scriptures that stands secure. It is still good to know in these days of international terrorism that God is with us and He is protecting us.

We moved back to Belfast in 1973 taking our little house church with us. God miraculously provided for us, giving us a large house in Ravenhill Park next door to the Ulster Rugby Grounds, at the ridiculously low rent of £10 per week.

The Belfast we moved back to, however, was very different from the one we left in 1970. By March '71 rioting in the city had escalated and rubber bullets and tear gas began to be used by the army on people who were using petrol bombs and nail bombs against them. The IRA had shot dead the first British soldier to be killed in the troubles. There was a high level of violence; shootings and bombings became a daily occurrence.

During this time our son Ian was born, a strapping lad weighing in at nine pounds eight ounces, another healthy gorgeous baby. Many of us in the fellowship now lived in and around Ravenhill Park and were within walking distance of each others homes. Tensions were quite high in the general community as the effects of terrorism from both sides became worse and worse. Not a day passed without a bombing or sectarian murder. The little church that I grew up in and where we had been married was razed to the ground and the hotel we had our wedding reception in was destroyed by a bomb, as were many other hotels and restaurants at that time with many fatalities.

In the middle of all the anxiety and fear those verses from Isaiah 54 kept coming back to me time and again:

*"You will have nothing to fear,
Terror will be far removed
It will not come near you"*

We did feel a measure of security in God's protection to the point that one Saturday morning we woke up to the sound of male voices calling up the stairs in our house. We had forgotten to lock our back door and finding the garage door open, two armed policemen had walked through the garage, round the back of the house and in through the back door into the front hall and were now checking to see that we were all safe!

These were days of great blessing for us as the Holy Spirit continued to move and we became the first house-church in Ireland. They were also dark days of extreme stress and trial as we lived through the worst times of the troubles.

In 1974 the Loyalists called for a 'workers strike' to bring out all the protestant workers right across the country, and over a period of many weeks the infrastructure of our society began to crumble. Workers at the main power stations cut levels of generating capacity and industry and commerce began to grind to a halt. There was limited petrol and therefore limited food in the supermarkets as lorries were unable to make deliveries. Milk, bread, and other staples were in short supply and eventually the power stations began to close down. Schools were closed and hospitals were limited to essential treatment and powered by generators.

Electricity supplies were limited to only a few hours per day. It was very frightening to move from a society where everything was in plentiful supply to one where within weeks I wondered if we would have enough food and heat for our children or if there would be medical help available in emergencies. We were also only allowed to use our phones in an emergency. Even now as I think about it I can feel something of the anxiety that we all experienced, especially the mothers.

During this time our little community really pulled together. As milk and fresh food were unable to be delivered to the shops much of it had to be dumped, some of our men would go out to the farms to find milk and potatoes which they would then share out with the community. Others would find different supplies including a little petrol and we would all make sure that everyone had enough to live on. Often in the evenings we would gather in each others homes with our children and play board games by candlelight. That was fun and very enlightening as we played Colditz and discovered how competitive most of us actually were. Our 'house-church' continued to bond together and grow numerically, spiritually and in love for one another.

The Ulster Workers Strike lasted for fifteen days and towards the end the power stations had come to almost complete shutdown. If they had completely shut down it would have taken six weeks to power them up again. It felt like what it must have been like in the very darkest days of the war. The strike had also unleashed a wave of sectarian murders against Roman Catholics who had tried to carry on working during the fifteen days.

In the middle of all this God spoke to us about how He was baptising Roman Catholics in the Holy Spirit just as He had with us. We duly began to attend ecumenical charismatic meetings at Queens University Chaplaincy in the centre of Belfast. I will never forget shaking hands for the first time with a Roman Catholic brother. It was a huge step for me coming from my Ulster protestant background where we had been segregated since childhood, but God was on the move. He very soon convicted us of the religious bigotry and prejudice that was a part of our blood-line, the superiority and racial pride that is at the heart of all prejudgment of people of different colour, race or religion from our own.

We truly repented and found ourselves forgiven, cleansed, and enjoying wonderful fellowship with our Spirit-filled Catholic brothers and sisters. Hugging nuns was a bit strange!

About this time we met Des Dick who led a Catholic Charismatic prayer group in a strong Republican area across the city in West Belfast. God quickly brought the two groups together. As we enjoyed fellowship we began to explore ways that we could come together more regularly. We found that the secret was to emphasise the truths and practices that united us and agree to differ about the others. Some of these things were political as well as scriptural.

Protestant Para-military groups were murdering innocent Catholics found in the wrong area at the wrong time and committing terrible atrocities. Protestants were also at great risk in Catholic areas. In the midst of all this 'Belfast Christian Family' was born, two thirds protestant and one third Roman Catholic, all baptised in the Holy Spirit and loving Jesus.

Part of the practical arrangements involved things like bussing people across the city to meet together in each other's areas. The joint leaders team also met together in both Catholic and Protestant homes. They often came home late as they had to wait until it was safe to travel across the city. I prayed a lot for their protection in those days. My husband was literally in danger of his life.

We shared together in our weddings, infant baptisms, infant dedications, and adult baptisms on the beach. We shared picnics, days out in the mountains and at the beach, and holiday conferences together. We once had a holiday 'Just for Joy' in the large castle at Castlewellan set in a beautiful forest park at the foot of the Mourne Mountains. By this time we were well established as an ecumenical community and were learning more and more about each other. There was a large lake in the park and David accidently dropped his car keys into it and couldn't find them.

One of the Catholic girls said: 'Ask St Anthony to help you, he is good at finding things that are lost.' This was completely new ground for us, we proddies didn't ask the saints for help but this time David did and picked his keys out of the lake immediately.

We had guests from England at the conference including John Noble, Gerald Coates, and Maurice Smith. One day John went into the town to buy some postage stamps. The man in the shop scratched his head and said, 'Stamps now, well I know I have some in a drawer here somewhere. Tell yez what, I'll ask the wife and if yez come back tomorrow ye can have them.'

We had wonderful 'Just for Joy' conferences in Donegal and at an ecumenical Centre in Ballycastle and these times were full of joy and humour. We were Irish after all!

I share a lot more of my own story in my book *In the Valley* but it has been a real joy and privilege to write this one, to spend time with old friends who have contributed their memories.

# FR. PETER HOCKEN MEMORIAL

Very sadly our dear friend Fr. Peter Hocken was called home to heaven during the night on June 10th 1917 only one week after attending the Golden Jubilee of the Catholic Charismatic Renewal in Rome attended by thousands of people from across the globe.

The Holy Father, Francis, invited him to this event and encouraged him to preach before the church about reconciliation among Christians which he did with obvious immense pleasure.

Back from Rome, Father Peter was full of joy and enthusiasm because he had been able to take part in this very significant event for the whole church and the entire world as prominent protestant pastors blessed Pope Francis and the Catholics, and prayers for forgiveness for sins perpetrated against Catholics and those perpetrated by Catholics against brothers and sisters from other denominations were offered in the ancient Roman stadium, Circus Maximus, the site of the martyrdom of so many early Christians.

Pope Francis quoted the prayer of Jesus in John 17:21:

'I pray also for those who will believe in me through their message, that all of them may be one, Father just as you are in me and I am in you.'

This prayer was the focus of Fr. Peter's life and ministry.

David had spent a night at his home in Hainburg on the Monday before the celebration enjoying a good old natter as they always did. Many of us had the privilege of attending his workshop in Rome which he shared with Fr. Cantamalessa the preacher to the papal household and a great advocate of Renewal.

Fr. Peter will be greatly missed by the wider church and also by many of us personally.

Further copies of this book, and also
Mary's book about her own journey
in Renewal, *In The Valley*,
are obtainable from:

**Goodnews Books**
**Upper Level**
**St. John the Apostle Church**
**296 Sundon Park Road**
**Luton, Beds. LU3 3AL**

www.goodnewsbooks.co.uk
orders@goodnewsbooks.co.uk
01582 571011